Student Activity Guide for

CHANGES & CHOICES

Personal Development & Relationships

by
Ruth E. Bragg, Ph.D.
Director of Spokane Area
Vocational Skills Center
Spokane, Washington

South Holland, Illinois
THE GOODHEART-WILLCOX COMPANY, INC.
Publishers

INTRODUCTION

This Student Activity Guide is designed for use with the text, *Changes and Choices: Personal Development and Relationships.* It will help you learn more about yourself and the changes that take place as you become an adult.

The activities in this guide are divided into chapters that correspond with the chapters in the text. By reading the text first, you will have the information you need to complete the activities. Try to complete the activities without referring to the text. If necessary, you can look at the book again later to complete any questions you could not answer. At that time, you can also compare the answers you have to the information in the book.

You will find a number of types of activities in this guide. Some of the activities, such as word mazes and crossword puzzles, have "right" answers. These activities can be used as review guides when you study for tests and quizzes. Other activities, such as case studies and surveys, will ask for opinions and reactions that cannot be judged as "right" or "wrong." These activities are designed to stimulate your thinking and help you apply information presented in the text.

The activities in this guide have been designed to increase your interest and understanding of the text material. The more thought you put into the activities, the more knowledge you will gain from them.

Copyright 1993

by

THE GOODHEART-WILLCOX COMPANY, INC.

Previous Edition Copyright 1986

International Standard Book Number 0-87006-983-7

2 3 4 5 6 7 8 9 10   93   97 96 95 94

CONTENTS

Part 3 ▶ GETTING ALONG WITH OTHERS

▼ Part 4 MANAGING YOUR RESOURCES

 **Chapter 1**

GROWING AND CHANGING

CHILDREN OR ADULTS?

Activity A

Chapter 1

Name _____

Date _____ Period _____

In small groups, discuss ways people show that they still think of adolescents as children. Also discuss ways people show that they have begun to think of adolescents as adults. Then complete the sentences and answer the questions below.

1. Adolescent guys feel they are being treated like children when:

    a. _____

    b. _____

    c. _____

2. Adolescent girls feel they are being treated like children when:

    a. _____

    b. _____

    c. _____

3. Adolescent guys feel they are being treated like adults when:

    a. _____

    b. _____

    c. _____

4. Adolescent girls feel they are being treated like adults when:

    a. _____

    b. _____

    c. _____

5. How do you prefer to be treated? _____

6. How can you encourage other people to treat you the way you want to be treated?

    _____

    _____

    _____

PHYSICAL GROWTH

Activity B

Chapter 1

Name _____

Date _____ Period _____

Complete the following chart outlining the changes that take place in different body systems due to physical changes during adolescence. Then answer the questions below.

	Function of system	Signs of growth during adolescence
Skeletal system		
Muscular system		
Reproductive system		Females: Males:

1. Why would it be inaccurate to say, "Puberty begins at age 12"? _____

_____

2. Give an example of a large muscle skill. _____

3. Give an example of a skill that requires eye-hand coordination._____

4. Name three factors that influence your growth and development.

_____

_____

_____

HANDLING EMOTIONS

Activity C

Chapter 1

Name _____

Date _____ Period _____

Write an ending to each of the following situations involving emotions.

1. Joe picks on the way Jim reads in English class. He makes fun of the way Jim throws the ball in gym class. He makes snide remarks about the grades Jim gets in math class, too. Joe's behavior makes Jim angry. How can Jim express his anger in a mature way? _____

_____

_____

_____

2. Marge, Nancy, and Lori all tried out for the lead role in the class play. The next day, the announcement was made that Nancy got the part. Lori and Marge are jealous. How can they handle their jealousy without damaging their friendship with Nancy? _____

_____

_____

_____

3. Nicholas has always done well in math class. Two weeks ago, however, his math teacher started teaching a geometry unit that Nicholas has had trouble understanding. Fear of failing the unit test this Friday is causing Nicholas to get headaches and lose sleep. How can Nicholas deal with his fear to help him relieve these symptoms? _____

_____

_____

_____

4. Jackson's parents' anniversary is next week. Jackson wants to show his parents that he cares for them, but he cannot afford to buy them a gift. How else can Jackson express his love for his parents? _____

_____

_____

_____

WHAT IS IMPORTANT TO YOU?

Activity D

Chapter 1

Name _____

Date _____ Period _____

Read the following statements. Place a check in the column that best describes your opinion. (There are no right or wrong answers.)

Agree Disagree Unsure

_____ _____ _____ 1. I want to own an expensive sports car someday.

_____ _____ _____ 2. I would rather watch television than study for an important test.

_____ _____ _____ 3. I think regularly attending religious services is important.

_____ _____ _____ 4. I like to wear all the lastest fashions.

_____ _____ _____ 5. I look forward to living on my own, earning my own income, paying my own bills, and making my own decisions.

_____ _____ _____ 6. I want to be rich.

_____ _____ _____ 7. I enjoy helping others whenever I can.

_____ _____ _____ 8. Spending time with my family is important to me.

_____ _____ _____ 9. I would be willing to fight for my country.

_____ _____ _____ 10. I like to buy the most modern appliances and gadgets.

_____ _____ _____ 11. I would rather have a few close friends than a lot of casual friends.

_____ _____ _____ 12. I try to look my best at all times.

_____ _____ _____ 13. I want to be a parent someday.

_____ _____ _____ 14. I want to go to college or trade school when I graduate from high school.

_____ _____ _____ 15. If necessary, I would harm another person to protect myself and my family.

What do your answers tell you about your values?

_____

_____

_____

_____

_____

_____

DAILY LEARNING

Activity E

Chapter 1

Name _____

Date _____ Period _____

Taking advantage of daily opportunities to learn is a sign of intellectual maturity. In the chart below, record something new that you learn each day for one week. Also explain how you gained this new knowledge. Then answer the questions at the bottom of the page.

MONDAY

What did you learn today? _____

_____

_____

How did you learn this? _____

_____

_____

TUESDAY

What did you learn today? _____

_____

_____

How did you learn this? _____

_____

_____

WEDNESDAY

What did you learn today? _____

_____

_____

How did you learn this? _____

_____

_____

THURSDAY

What did you learn today? _____

_____

_____

How did you learn this? _____

_____

_____

FRIDAY

What did you learn today? _____

_____

_____

How did you learn this? _____

_____

_____

SATURDAY

What did you learn today? _____

_____

How did you learn this? _____

_____

SUNDAY

What did you learn today? _____

_____

How did you learn this? _____

_____

1. Which of the things you learned did you find most interesting? _____
   Why? _____

   _____

2. Which of the vehicles of learning did you find most enjoyable? _____
   Why? _____

   _____

── GROWTH AND DEVELOPMENT CROSSWORD ──

Activity F

Chapter 1

Name _____

Date _____ Period _____

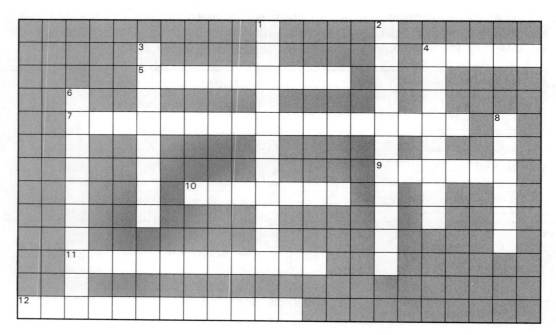

Across

4. People in the same age group are called _____.

5. An increasing ability to handle feelings is the result of _____ growth.

7. A skill or behavior that should be learned at a certain life stage is called a _____.

9. Development in a person's relationships with other people is known as _____ growth.

10. The time when the body changes in ways that makes it possible to produce children is called _____.

11. People, objects, and conditions that surround a person form that person's _____.

12. Development of a person's ability to learn is called _____ growth.

Down

1. _____ is the stage of life between childhood and adulthood.

2. A large amount of growth that occurs in a short period of time is a _____ _____.

3. _____ refers to all the traits that are passed at birth to a person from his or her ancestors.

4. _____ growth is seen as changes that happen to the body due to development.

6. A person who is in the stage of life between childhood and adulthood is called an _____.

8. _____ are objects and ideas that are important to a person.

Chapter 2 ▼ MAKING DECISIONS

CHANCE DECISIONS

Activity A

Chapter 2

Name _____

Date _____ Period _____

Read the following story and answer the questions below.

Colleen is the president of the drama club. She has to choose one of two club members to be the student director of the winter play.

Mark Meyers
- Has been in the club three years.
- Has had small roles in three past plays.
- Elective courses include acting and an English course on American playwrights.
- Other activities include membership on the debate team and student council.

Melvin Olson (Colleen's boyfriend)
- Has been in the club one year.
- Worked on stage crew for one play.
- Elective courses include automotive technology and art.
- Other activities include marching band and science club.

Colleen could not decide who to choose to direct the winter play. She left the decision to the flip of a coin.

1. Pretend you are Colleen. Flip a coin to see who you would choose to direct the play.

   Heads (Mark) _____   Tails (Melvin) _____

2. How could this decision affect Colleen? _____

   _____

3. How could this decision affect the play? _____

   _____

4. Flip a coin 10 times and tally the results below.

   Heads _____   Tails _____

5. Do you think flipping a coin is a good way to make a decision? _____

   Why or why not? _____

   _____

DECISION-MAKING STEPS

Name _____

Date _____ Period _____

Work in small groups to label each of the following examples with the appropriate step of the decision-making process. Discuss why the process would be incomplete without each step.

Step ____. _____ _____ I will buy the store brand.	Step ____. _____ _____ Store brand. Generic brand. National brand.
Step ____. _____ _____ Purchase, prepare, and eat the pizza I've chosen.	Step ____. _____ _____ The generic brand is inexpensive but does not have enough sauce or cheese. The store brand is reasonably priced and has enough sauce and cheese. The national brand is expensive but has extra sauce and cheese.
Step ____. _____ _____ I feel I made a good decision. I saved money over the national brand. I also got more sauce and cheese than the generic brand.	Step ____. _____ _____ Which brand of pizza should I buy?

BUYING DECISIONS

Activity C

Chapter 2

Name _____

Date _____ Period _____

As a consumer, using the decision-making process can help you budget your time and money wisely. Use the following chart to compare different forms of orange juice. Then work through the steps of the decision-making process to make a decision about which form you would buy.

FORM	COST PER SERVING	TIME TO PREPARE
Fresh oranges		
Frozen concentrate		
Ready-to-serve		

1. State the decision you must make.

_____

2. List your alternatives.

_____ _____ _____

3. Think about the results of each alternative.

	PROS:	CONS:
Fresh	_____	_____
Frozen	_____	_____
Ready-to-serve	_____	_____

4. Choose one of the alternatives. Why did you make this choice?

_____

5. Carry out your decision by tasting the juice you selected.

6. Evaluate your decision. Did you like your choice? Would you make the same choice again? Why or why not?

_____

_____

VALUES AND DECISION MAKING

Read the following decision-making situations. Then answer the questions about how values might affect the decisions being made.

1. Cynthia is a good math student. Her best friend, Janet, does not do well in math. Janet is afraid of failing the math test tomorrow. She wants to copy the answers from Cynthia's test. How could the following values limit Cynthia's decision to let her friend copy her answers?

   Honesty: _____

   Friendship: _____

   Self-respect: _____

2. Each summer, Mario and his family take a vacation together. Mario has a close relationship with his family so he always looks forward to the trip. This year, money is tight. Mario's family decided that a camping trip is the only kind of vacation they will be able to afford. Mario knows that he will have to pay for his own share of the trip. Yesterday, Mario's friend, Rick, invited Mario to join him and his family on a trip to Disneyland. Rick's parents would pay for all of Mario's expenses. However, the Disneyland trip and the camping trip are scheduled for the same week. Therefore, Mario must decide which trip he will take. How could the following values limit Mario's decision?

   Family: _____

   Friendship: _____

   Travel: _____

   Money: _____

3. Roxanne's friend, Tina, is having a party Saturday night. The party would be the perfect place for Roxanne to show off her new sweater. It would also be a good chance for her to get to know Tony, the new guy in her science class. This afternoon, a woman for whom Roxanne often baby-sits called to see if Roxanne could baby-sit Saturday night. After buying the sweater, Roxanne needs the money she could earn from baby-sitting. She also does not want to risk losing a loyal customer. What values might limit Roxanne's decision about what to do on Saturday night? _____

   _____

   _____

   _____

   _____

   _____

LIMITS TO ALTERNATIVES

Activity E

Chapter 2

Name _____

Date _____ Period _____

Suppose you are trying to decide what you might do when you finish high school. Consider your alternatives as you answer the following questions.

1. What is one of your skills? _____

   What alternative would be open to you because of this skill? _____

2. What is a skill that you lack? _____

   What alternative would not be available to you due to this lack of skill? _____

3. What is your attitude about going to college? _____

   What alternative would not be available to you because of this attitude? _____

4. What standards do you have regarding work training? _____

   What alternative would not be available to you because of these standards?

   _____

5. Describe the opportunities for employment in your area. _____

   What alternatives for employment would not be available to you if you wished to work locally?

   _____

6. What person do you believe will have the greatest influence on your future?

   _____

   How might this person limit your alternatives as you decide what to do after high school?

   _____

7. What physical needs will you have to provide for yourself as an adult that someone else is

   currently providing for you? _____

   How will meeting these needs limit your alternatives as you decide what to do after high school?

   _____

8. What is one of your greatest values? _____

   How could this value limit your alternatives as you decide what to do after high school?

   _____

9. What is one of your materialistic goals? _____

   How could achieving this goal limit your alternatives as you decide what to do after high school?

   _____

10. What is one of your nonmaterialistic goals? _____

    How could achieving this goal limit your alternatives as you decide what to do after high school?

    _____

DECISION-MAKING CROSSWORD

Activity F
Chapter 2

Name _____

Date _____ Period _____

Across

1. Fourth step in the decision-making process that makes your decision happen.
2. An option you can choose when making a decision.
5. Second step in the decision-making process that allows you to see all your options.
7. The choice you make.
9. The last step in the decision-making process.
10. First step in the decision-making process when you identify what you are deciding.

Down

1. A result of a decision.
3. Third step in the decision-making process when you consider the possible results of your decision.
4. Careful decisions are made by following a step-by-step _____.
6. Skills, attitudes, and standards are inner _____ that can affect your decisions.
8. Fifth step in the decision-making process that allows you to find out if you have made a wise choice. (Two words.)

Chapter 3 — YOUR PERSONALITY

───────── PERSONALITY TRAIT CHECKLIST ─────────

Activity A

Name _____

Chapter 3

Date _____ Period _____

Check all of the personality traits listed below that you think describe yourself.

_____ Self-disciplined	_____ Happy
_____ Friendly	_____ Sad
_____ Shy	_____ Funny
_____ Intelligent	_____ Witty
_____ Thoughtful	_____ Boring
_____ Active	_____ Dependable
_____ Ambitious	_____ Unreliable
_____ Generous	_____ Tolerant
_____ Greedy	_____ Jealous
_____ Aggressive	_____ Capable
_____ Assertive	_____ Lazy
_____ Independent	_____ Moody
_____ Dependent	_____ Nervous
_____ Talkative	_____ Patient
_____ Loyal	_____ Cruel
_____ Honest	_____ Kind
_____ Dishonest	_____ Religious
_____ Crabby	_____ Respectful
_____ Pleasant	_____ Sarcastic
_____ Extrovert	_____ Helpful
_____ Introvert	_____ Selfish
_____ Ambivert	_____ Other _____
_____ Self-confident	_____ Other _____

1. Do you think a close friend would choose the same list of traits to describe you? Why or why not?

_____

_____

2. Do you think someone who had just met you would choose the same list of traits to describe you? Why or why not? _____

_____

PERSONALITY DEVELOPMENT

Activity B

Chapter 3

Name _____

Date _____ Period _____

Ask one of your parents to list five personality traits that would describe you as an infant. Write his or her responses in the first column below. In the second column, identify whether or not that trait still describes you. Then look at the list of environmental factors listed below the chart. Explain how each of these factors has affected your development of the personality traits listed in the first column.

HEREDITY (Personality traits as an infant)	ENVIRONMENT (Traits that still describe you)

1. Home and family. _____

   _____

   _____

2. School, classmates, and teachers. _____

   _____

   _____

3. Neighborhood and neighbors. _____

   _____

   _____

4. The region where you live. _____

   _____

   _____

BUILDING SELF-CONCEPT

Activity C

Chapter 3

Name _____

Date _____ Period _____

Create a comic strip about forming a positive self-concept. Complete the story about Mike and his father started in the first frame below. Follow the instructions below each frame.

How do you think this experience affected Mike's self-concept?

Illustrate an experience on the fishing trip that might cause Mike to form a negative self-concept.

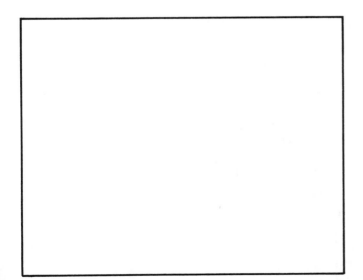

Show how Mike's reaction to this experience kept him from forming a negative self-concept.

Show how Mike's father's reaction to this experience helped Mike build a positive self-concept.

Activity D

Chapter 3

Name _____

Date _____ Period _____

Complete the following statements describing the different parts of your personality.

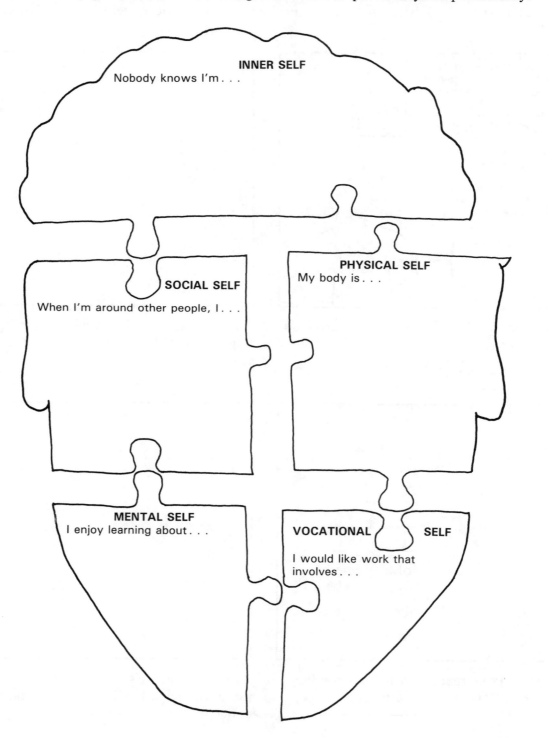

INNER SELF
Nobody knows I'm . . .

SOCIAL SELF
When I'm around other people, I . . .

PHYSICAL SELF
My body is . . .

MENTAL SELF
I enjoy learning about . . .

VOCATIONAL SELF
I would like work that involves . . .

ROOM FOR IMPROVEMENT

Activity E   Name _____

Chapter 3   Date _____ Period _____

Read the following situations and answer the questions that follow.

1. Some people think Omar is a snob because he never talks to anybody. Actually, Omar feels nervous around people he doesn't know. He's afraid to talk to them because he's afraid they will not be interested in what he has to say.

   How would you describe Omar's personality?_____

   What suggestions would you give Omar if he wanted to change his personality?

   _____

   _____

   _____

2. Wherever Walter goes, he seems to have a crowd of people with him. He won't go to a school dance with just one or two friends; he goes with eight or ten! Last week, Walter missed seeing his favorite band because he couldn't find anyone to go with him.

   How would you describe Walter's personality? _____

   What suggestions would you give Walter if he wanted to change his personality?

   _____

   _____

   _____

3. Susan badgered everyone into voting for her to be president of her scout troop. Now, she always insists that the group do things her way. She bosses the other members around and puts down their ideas.

   How would you describe Susan's personality? _____

   What suggestions would you give Susan if she wanted to change her personality?

   _____

   _____

   _____

4. Gretchen spends most of her time by herself. She doesn't dislike people, and she's not afraid to meet them. She simply prefers being alone reading books, sewing, or writing in her journal.

   How would you describe Gretchen's personality? _____

   What suggestions would you give Gretchen if she wanted to change her personality?

   _____

   _____

   _____

(Continued)

5. Ralph has trouble letting other people know how he feels. When he disagrees with a friend, he usually keeps his opinion to himself. When someone cuts in front of him in line, he doesn't say anything. When he gets stuck doing his sister's chores, he just puts up with it quietly.

How would you describe Ralph's personality? _____

What suggestions would you give Ralph if he wanted to change his personality?

_____

_____

_____

6. What personality trait would you like to change about yourself? _____

Why would you like to change this trait? _____

_____

How might you go about making this change? _____

_____

_____

How long do you think it might take you to make this change? _____

THE ROLES YOU PLAY

── TRADITIONAL AND NONTRADITIONAL ROLES ──

Activity A   Name _____

Chapter 4   Date _____ Period _____

Discuss the following situations in small groups. Role-play one of them for the class. Then write your reactions to the questions below.

1. Tracy often joined her older brothers in neighborhood football games when she was younger. When she started eighth grade, Tracy wanted to try out for the JV football team. When she talked to the coach, however, he said girls shouldn't be allowed to play football.

   How might this situation be different if Tracy were a guy?

   _____

   _____

   What kind of stereotypes does the coach have about girls?

   _____

   Do you think Tracy should be allowed to fill a nontraditional role as a female member of a football team? Why or Why not?

   _____

   _____

   What would be an example of a traditional role that Tracy might fill at school?

   _____

2. William was swinging on one of the swings in the park. His mother came over to him and said, "William, get off of that swing. Swings are for kids."

   How might this situation be different if William were younger?

   _____

   _____

   What kind of stereotypes does William's mother have about teenagers?

   _____

   Do you think William should be allowed to pursue this nontraditional role activity? Why or why not?

   _____

   _____

   What would be an example of a traditional role activity that William might do in the park?

   _____

(Continued)

3. Dennis answered an ad in the paper about a baby-sitting job. However, the woman with whom he spoke said she wanted to hire a girl to watch her children.

   How might this situation be different if Dennis were a girl?

   _____

   _____

   What kind of stereotypes does the woman have about guys?

   _____

   Do you think Dennis should be allowed to fill a nontraditional role as a male baby-sitter? Why or why not?

   _____

   _____

   What would be an example of a traditional employee role that Dennis might fill?

   _____

4. Flo's band director didn't like her idea of holding a concert and banquet for the parents of the band members. He said he didn't want to be bothered with all the planning. Flo said she would do the planning. However, he said she was too young to take care of all the details needed to organize such an event.

   How might this situation be different if Flo were older?

   _____

   _____

   What kind of stereotypes does the band director have about teenagers?

   _____

   Do you think Flo should be given this nontraditional role responsibility? Why or why not?

   _____

   _____

   What would be an example of a traditional role responsibility Flo might be given in the band?

   _____

WHAT ARE YOUR ROLES?

Activity B

Chapter 4

Name _____

Date _____ Period _____

Indicate which of the following roles you fill. Put an "O" beside the roles you choose to fill. Put an "X" beside the roles that you do not get to choose. Then answer the questions below.

_____ son

_____ daughter

_____ friend

_____ leader

_____ student

_____ sister

_____ brother

_____ citizen

_____ grandchild

_____ club member

_____ religious follower

_____ youngest child

_____ middle child

_____ oldest child

_____ only child

_____ neighbor

_____ employee

_____ cousin

_____ band member

_____ dating partner

_____ niece

_____ nephew

_____ team member

_____ consumer

_____ choir member

_____ scout

_____ other _____

_____ other _____

_____ other _____

_____ other _____

1. Give an example of an assigned role you have in your family and explain why you were assigned that role. _____

_____

_____

2. Aside from friend, what other roles do you have in your peer group? _____

_____

3. Describe the role expectations other people have for you in one of the roles you checked above.

_____

_____

_____

4. Describe any problems you might have with role conflict and explain how you would handle them. _____

_____

_____

LEARNING ABOUT ROLES

Complete the following statements about roles. Then arrange the circled letters to spell a term related to learning about roles.

1. Friend, team member, and dating partner are all examples of ___ ___ ___ ___

   ___ ___ ___ ___ ___ roles.

2. Your ___ ___ ___ ___ ___ ___ ___ ___ affects people's role expectations of you.

3. A ___ ___ ___ is a pattern of behavior.

4. ___ ___ ___ ___ ___ ___ , such as education and honesty, affect the role expectations of family members and peers.

5. Many family roles are ___ ___ ___ ___ ___ ___ ___ ___ ___ roles.

6. Anyone who uses goods and services is filling the role of a

   ___ ___ ___ ___ ___ ___ ___ .

7. Student, religious follower, and employee are all examples of

   ___ ___ ___ ___ ___ ___ ___ ___ roles.

8. ___ ___ ___ ___ ___ ___ ___ ___ ___ ___ roles are roles that have commonly been filled by certain groups throughout history.

9. Role ___ ___ ___ ___ ___ ___ ___ ___ ___ ___ involves becoming aware of your roles and making the most of them.

10. Sports figures and TV stars often become ___ ___ ___ ___ ___ ___ ___ ___ ___ for teens who admire them.

11. Traditional roles are often based on ___ ___ ___ ___ ___ ___ ___ ___ ___ ___ .

12. Daughter, brother, and nephew are all examples of ___ ___ ___ ___ ___ roles.

Circled letters: _____

You may suffer from ___ ___ ___ ___ ___ ___ ___ ___ ___ ___ ___ ___ when one of your roles prevents you from filling some of your other roles.

Chapter 5 FAMILIES

——————— FAMILY STRUCTURES ———————

Activity A

Chapter 5

Name _____

Date _____ Period _____

Define family structure. Then match each of the following statements with the family structure to which it applies.

Family structure: _____

_____

a. Nuclear family.
b. Extended family.
c. Single-parent family.
d. Blended family.

_____ 1. Several generations of family members may live together in this family structure.

_____ 2. The most popular family structure in America.

_____ 3. This structure may include almost any combination of parents, children, aunts, uncles, cousins, and grandparents.

_____ 4. This structure may be formed due to death, divorce, or separation.

_____ 5. This structure is formed when the parent in a single-parent family marries.

_____ 6. Other relatives live with members of a nuclear family in this structure.

_____ 7. This structure may include two stepparents and several stepchildren.

_____ 8. One parent lives with his or her children in this structure.

_____ 9. This structure is made up of a married couple who may or may not have children.

_____ 10. A parent in this structure cannot share daily child care responsibilities with a spouse.

_____ 11. Parents in this family structure want their children to be able to get along with new stepbrothers and stepsisters.

_____ 12. This structure includes at least one stepparent and one stepchild.

_____ 13. This family structure was more common in the past.

_____ 14. A couple who begin married life living with the parents of the bride or groom live in this structure.

_____ 15. Parents in this family structure want to help their children accept new stepparents.

_____ 16. A parent who has never married lives in this structure.

FAMILY LIFE CYCLE

Name _____

Date _____ Period _____

Label the time line below with the stages of the family life cycle. Describe the event that signals the beginning of each stage in the space provided. Then answer the questions below.

  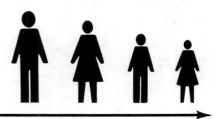

_____ Stage   _____ Stage   _____ Stage

begins when: _____   begins when: _____   begins when: _____

_____   _____   _____

_____   _____   _____

_____   _____   _____

_____ Stage   _____ Stage

begins when: _____   begins when: _____

_____   _____

_____   _____

_____   _____

1. What causes the family life cycle to vary from family to family? _____

_____

2. Give an example of how a family would skip a stage in the family life cycle._____

_____

3. Give an example of how a family would overlap stages in the family life cycle._____

_____

4. Give an example of how a family would repeat a stage in the family life cycle._____

_____

FAMILY FUNCTIONS

Activity C

Chapter 5

Name _____

Date _____ Period _____

Read the following story. Then list the four major functions of the family on the lines below. Give at least two examples of how each function is being fulfilled by the family in the story.

At noon on Saturdays, Carrie's family always eats lunch together. Today, as Carrie entered the kitchen, she found her father feeding strained carrots to her baby sister. Carrie's mother came up from the laundry room in the basement and set a basket of clean clothes on the counter. Just then, Carrie's younger brother, Sean, came running into the house. Sean's clothes were muddy and he had a cut on his right hand.

"Sean, what happened to you?" his mother asked.

"I was playing baseball and I had to slide into third base," Sean replied. "Aside from the slide, today's game wasn't very good. A couple of kids got into a fight. Some other kids were arguing with the umpire. One guy even quit right in the middle of the game."

"That's a shame," his mother said. "I hope you never behave that way. It's important to follow the rules and be a good sport. Now let me take a look at that hand." She washed out the cut and bandaged Sean's hand.

"How could you play baseball?" Carrie asked her brother. "I thought you didn't have a glove."

"I borrowed yours," Sean answered.

"What makes you think you can just use my glove whenever you want without asking?" Carrie demanded.

"Carrie has a point," her father said to Sean. "You should ask your sister for permission when you want to borrow her belongings." Then he turned to Carrie and continued, "You must be willing to share with Sean. I'm proud of his skill in baseball. I don't want him to have to stop playing just because he doesn't have a glove."

"Okay, Sean," Carrie agreed. "I realize that you can't play baseball without a glove. I guess you can use mine as long as you remember to ask first."

"Thanks, Carrie!" Sean said. "I'll remember!"

1. Function: _____

   Examples: _____

   _____

2. Function: _____

   Examples: _____

   _____

3. Function: _____

   Examples: _____

   _____

4. Function: _____

   Examples: _____

   _____

FAMILY RIGHTS AND RESPONSIBILITIES

Activity D

Chapter 5

Name _____

Date _____ Period _____

Write a Bill of Rights for family members. Beside each right, write a corresponding responsibility. Then answer the questions below.

BILL OF RIGHTS

1. _____
   _____
2. _____
   _____
3. _____
   _____
4. _____
   _____
5. _____
   _____
6. _____
   _____
7. _____
   _____
8. _____

RESPONSIBILITIES

1. _____
   _____
2. _____
   _____
3. _____
   _____
4. _____
   _____
5. _____
   _____
6. _____
   _____
7. _____
   _____
8. _____

1. What kinds of household chores do you share with your family members?

   _____

2. What kinds of goals do you and your family members have?

   _____

3. How do you help care for your family's belongings?

   _____

4. What do you do to make getting along with your family easier?

   _____

NEW TRADITIONS FROM OLD

Activity E

Chapter 5

Name _____

Date _____ Period _____

Discuss the case study below in a small group. Then write your ideas for forming a new tradition from two old ones.

Janet and her family celebrate Christmas the same way their friends and neighbors do. They decorate evergreen trees. They shop for gifts. They go to church services. They go caroling. They bake cookies. On Christmas Eve, they hang stockings and wait for Santa Claus to bring them presents. On Christmas Day, they eat a feast of turkey, dressing, mashed potatoes, cranberry sauce, and lots of pies and cakes.

This year, Lucianna, an exchange student from Italy, is living with Janet and her family. In Italy, instead of decorating an evergreen, Lucianna's family trims an olive tree with oranges. They fast on December 23. On Christmas Eve, they recite poems before a manger scene. Then at sunset, they light fireworks and break their fast with a feast of macaroni, eel, and stuffed capon. Lucianna doesn't hang a stocking for Santa Claus on Christmas Eve. Instead, she puts out her shoes on the evening of January 5. Then she waits for La Befana, an old woman dressed in rags, to fill them with ashes or gifts.

How can Janet and Lucianna combine their family Christmas traditions to make this holiday season special for both of them? _____

_____

_____

_____

_____

Describe a tradition that your family follows. _____

_____

_____

_____

How did this tradition get started? _____

_____

_____

_____

How long have you been following this tradition? _____

_____

Would you like to continue this tradition with your own family someday? _____

FAMILY WORD SCRAMBLE

Name _____

Date _____ Period _____

Unscramble the letters below. Then use the words to complete the following statements about families.

NNERETSGIAO = _ _ _ _ _ _ _ _ _ _ _

IFEL LCCYE = _ _ _ _ _ _ _ _ _

YLAMFI = _ _ _ _ _ _

USRCTTRUE = _ _ _ _ _ _ _ _ _

IUNTSFONC = _ _ _ _ _ _ _ _ _

APDINNXGE = _ _ _ _ _ _ _ _ _

CLOATSIIOIZNA = _ _ _ _ _ _ _ _ _ _ _ _ _

DRITITNOA = _ _ _ _ _ _ _ _ _

XEEEDDNT = _ _ _ _ _ _ _ _

NISEGL-ARPTNE = _ _ _ _ _ _ _-_ _ _ _ _ _

LOASG = _ _ _ _ _

RORNIPACTOE = _ _ _ _ _ _ _ _ _ _ _

ACHINNGLU = _ _ _ _ _ _ _ _ _

BLEDDEN = _ _ _ _ _ _ _

1. When the first child arrives, a family enters the _____ stage of the family life cycle.

2. In a _____-_____ family, one parent lives with his or her children.

3. Procreation, physical care of members, emotional support of members, and socialization of children are all _____ of the family

4. When the first child leaves home, the _____ stage of the family life cycle begins.

5. Family members have a responsibility to help each other meet _____.

6. Several _____ of family members may live together in an extended family.

7. A family _____ is defined according to the members who are in the family group.

8. An _____ family may include almost any combination of parents, children, aunts, uncles, cousins, and grandparents.

9. A family _____ is an activity that takes on special meaning for family members as it is done repeatedly over time.

10. As families change, they go through stages of a family _____ _____.

11. A _____ family includes at least one stepparent and one stepchild.

12. _____ is the bearing of children.

13. A group of two or more people who are related by blood, marriage, or adoption is a _____.

14. Teaching children to fit into society is known as _____.

Chapter 6 ▾ PARENTS AS PEOPLE

————— RESPONSIBILITIES OF PARENTS —————

Activity A   Name _____

Chapter 6   Date _____ Period _____

Define parents: _____

_____

List responsibilities parents have as they raise their children:

1. _____
2. _____
3. _____
4. _____
5. _____
6. _____
7. _____
8. _____
9. _____
10. _____

In the chart below, describe how each family structure might affect the way parents carry out their responsibilities.

Family structure	Affect on responsibilities of parents
Nuclear family	
Foster family	
Extended family	
Single-parent family	
Blended family	

MIDDLE AGE SURVEY

Name _____

Date _____ Period _____

Survey five middle-aged people about the changes and concerns that are affecting them as they grow older. Record their answers in the chart provided. Compile your results and report your findings to class.

1. Your sex: a. Male.   b. Female.

2. Your age: _____

3. Which of the following health concerns has begun to trouble you as you have grown older? (You may choose more than one response.)
   a. I have had no new health concerns. b. Stiff joints.   c. Weak bones.   d. Heart disease.
   e. High blood pressure.   f. Weight gain.   g. Weakened vision.   h. Other health concerns:

   _____

4. Are you careful to watch your calorie intake and eat a balanced diet?   a. Yes.   b. No.

5. How often do you exercise? a. 1-2 times a week. b. 3-4 times a week. c. Daily. d. Not at all.

6. Which of the following physical changes have you noticed related to your appearance as you have grown older? (You may choose more than one response.) a. I have notices no changes in my appearance. b. Graying hair.   c. Hair loss.   d. Wrinkle lines around the mouth.
   e. Wrinkle lines around the eyes.   f. Other changes in appearance:_____

7. Have you ever used any dyes, creams, or other products to help you hide the signs of aging?
   a. Yes.   b. No.

8. Which of the following emotions have you experienced as you have grown older? (You may choose more than one response.)   a. Depression over the loss of your youth.   b. Enjoyment of freedom from child care tasks.   c. Fear of the approach of old age.   d. Anticipation of retirement.   e. Envy of the vigor of younger people.   f. Satisfaction with financial stability.
   g. Sadness over the loss of a friend or spouse.   h. Loneliness as children leave home.
   i. Other emotions: _____

9. As the number of time-consuming parenting tasks decrease, how do you use your extra free time? a. Spending more time with a favorite hobby.   b. Learning a new skill or interest.
   c. Taking a class or returning to school.   d. Traveling.   e. Other leisure-time activities:

   _____

(Continued)

10. How do you feel about your work role?   a. Satisfied.   b. Desire a change.   c. I'm retired.

11. In what ways are you involved in your community? (You may choose more than one response.)
a. Being a member of a civic group.   b. Doing volunteer work.   c. Running for public office.
d. Keeping abreast of current events.   e. Voting in local elections.   f. Supporting my child's
membership in school or community groups.   g. Other community involvement: _____

12. Has growing older had an effect on your relationship with your spouse?   a. Yes.   b. No.

13. Are you a grandparent?   a. Yes.   b. No.

14. Which of the following changes of housing have you experienced or will you experience as
you grow older?   a. No change of housing.   b. Move to a smaller home.   c. Move to a retirement community.   d. Move to a nursing home.   e. Move in with children or other relatives.

SURVEY RESPONSES

QUESTION	PERSON 1	PERSON 2	PERSON 3	PERSON 4	PERSON 5
1.					
2.					
3.					
4.					
5.					
6.					
7.					
8.					
9.					
10.					
11.					
12.					
13.					
14.					

THE GRANDPARENTS' CLUB

Imagine you are starting a business called The Grandparents' Club. The club is intended to help older people adjust to changes associated with aging. Complete the sentences below to help you design a creative brochure describing the services your business offers.

Noticing a little more gray hair and a few more lines on your face when you look in the mirror? At **The Grandparents' Club,** we help you adjust to the physical signs of aging by...

_____

_____

Feeling a little more stiffness in the joints or racking up a few more pounds on the scale lately? At **The Grandparents' Club,** we help you adjust to the health concerns of aging by...

_____

_____

Wondering what to do with all your free time now that you're retired? At **The Grandparents' Club,** we offer...

_____

_____

Considering new housing options now that the kids have moved away? At **The Grandparents' Club,** you'll find...

_____

_____

Have you recently lost a friend or loved one? At **The Grandparents' Club,** we can help you adjust to death by...

_____

_____

Not getting all you want out of your relationships with your grandchildren? At **The Grandparents' Club,** you and your grandchildren can...

_____

_____

DIFFERENT VIEWS

Activity D

Chapter 6

Name _____

Date _____ Period _____

In the chart below, list issues that often seem to cause conflict between teens and parents. In the left column, write the list from a teen's point of view. In the right column, write the list from a parent's point of view. Then answer the questions that follow.

TEEN VIEWPOINT	PARENTAL VIEWPOINT

1. What kinds of differences do you see between the two lists? _____

_____

2. Why do you think parents and teens seem to differ on these issues?_____

_____

3. How can teens deal with or eliminate these sources of conflict in their relationships with their

   parents? _____

_____

4. What might parents do to help their teenagers better understand and accept their viewpoints

   on these issues? _____

_____

CHANGING RELATIONSHIPS

Activity E

Chapter 6

Name _____

Date _____ Period _____

Discuss the following situations in small groups. Write your reactions to the questions about relationships between parents and teens. Then role-play one of the situations for the class.

1. When Geri was young, she was content to wear the clothes her mother bought for her. Now that she's in junior high, however, Geri is more aware of fashion trends. She wants to wear the latest clothing fads that her friends are wearing.

   Geri's mother says she can't afford to buy clothes that will be out of fashion in a few months. Geri has started baby-sitting to earn the money to buy the fads for herself.

   What do you think Geri's willingness to work for her own money says about her? _____
   _____

   How do you think her mother will feel about Geri working and buying her own clothes?
   _____

2. Tony has a 10 p.m. curfew on school nights. Last Thursday, Tony can home at 10:30 p.m. When he opened the door, Tony said, "Mom, Dad, I'm home. Sorry I'm late. I lost track of the time."

   What does Tony's forgetfulness say about him?_____
   _____

   What do you think might have gone through Tony's parents' minds when their son was not home at 10 p.m.? _____
   _____

   How do you think Tony's parents reacted when Tony came home? _____
   _____

3. Carmen's father thinks that young ladies should always wear dresses to school.

   How do you think he will react when Carmen tells him that she wants to wear jeans to school?
   _____

   _____

   How do you think Carmen should deal with her father's reaction? _____
   _____

   _____

SIBLINGS

—————————— SIBLING RELATIONSHIPS ——————————

Activity A

Chapter 7

Name _____

Date _____ Period _____

Read the following case study:

Beth is 13 years old. She and her 10-year-old brother, Eugene, live with their parents in a house in the suburbs. Beth does not spend a lot of time playing with Eugene. She spends most of her time with girls her age who live in the neighborhood. When Beth and Eugene do go places together, she always watches him carefully. She feels responsible for his safety so she tends to mother him.

Evaluate how each of the following changes in the case study might affect the sibling relationship described above.

1. Beth's parents are divorced. She and Eugene live with their mother in a house in the suburbs.

_____

_____

2. There are four other siblings in Beth's family. Her older brother, Robert, is 16 years old. Connie is nine, Caroline is eight, and Janet is four. All the children live with both parents in a house in the suburbs. (Describe only how this situation would affect Beth's relationship with Eugene.)

_____

_____

3. Beth and Eugene are spaced seven years apart. Eugene is only six years old. They both live with their parents in a house in the suburbs.

_____

_____

4. Instead of a younger brother, Beth has a 10-year old sister, Esther. Beth and Esther live with their parents in a house in the suburbs.

_____

_____

5. Beth and Eugene live with their parents in a house in the country. Their nearest neighbors live half a mile away.

_____

_____

BIRTH ORDER

Name _____

Date _____ Period _____

Read each of the statements below. Then place an X in the proper column to identify the birth order of the child described.

	Firstborn Child	Youngest Child	Middle Child	Only Child
1. May feel excluded.				
2. Independence and self-confidence may prompt this child to be a leader in his or her family.				
3. May be independent.				
4. May achieve success in school due to strong self-concept.				
5. May be given more freedom by parents than older siblings.				
6. May become a peacemaker among friends and family members.				
7. May be given more responsibilities than other siblings.				
8. May receive care from older siblings as well as from parents.				
9. May be less independent because other family members make many of this child's decisions.				
10. May feel lonely.				
11. May acquire special skills in an effort to gain attention and praise.				
12. May be like an only child after older siblings leave home.				
13. May be like an only child during first years of life.				
14. May learn fast due to extra attention from parents.				
15. May be pushed by parents to learn new skills.				

SIBLING SEX ROLES

Activity C

Chapter 7

Name _____

Date _____ Period _____

Read the list below. Suppose you have an older brother and an older sister. Indicate in the left column which one you think would do each task for you. Suppose you also have a younger brother and a younger sister. Indicate in the right column the one for which you would do each task. (You may indicate neither or both siblings for each item.)

OLDER SIBLINGS			YOUNGER SIBLINGS	
Brother	Sister		Brother	Sister
_____	_____	Help sibling with homework.	_____	_____
_____	_____	Share secrets with sibling.	_____	_____
_____	_____	Help sibling make friends.	_____	_____
_____	_____	Teach sibling how to cook.	_____	_____
_____	_____	Set a good example for sibling.	_____	_____
_____	_____	Understand sibling's feelings.	_____	_____
_____	_____	Teach sibling how to play ball.	_____	_____
_____	_____	Provide sibling with companionship.	_____	_____
_____	_____	Tease sibling.	_____	_____
_____	_____	Protect sibling from danger.	_____	_____
_____	_____	Lend clothes, bicycle, or other items to sibling.	_____	_____
_____	_____	Take sibling to a movie.	_____	_____
_____	_____	Show affection for sibling.	_____	_____
_____	_____	Give sibling advice about members of the opposite sex.	_____	_____
_____	_____	Help sibling solve problems with parents.	_____	_____
_____	_____	Help sibling make decisions about the future.	_____	_____
_____	_____	Argue with sibling.	_____	_____
_____	_____	Boss sibling about doing his or her chores.	_____	_____
_____	_____	Take sibling shopping.	_____	_____
_____	_____	Stick up for sibling.	_____	_____

HANDLING CONFLICT

Activity D

Chapter 7

Name _____

Date _____ Period _____

Discuss each of the following situations with members of a small group. Together, come up with a suggestion for solving each of the conflicts in a positive way.

1. Maja's sister, Tonya, is a state champion ice skater. Maja is proud of her sister's talent. However, she also envies all the time and attention Tonya gets from their parents. Lately, Maja has stopped going to Tonya's skating competitions. Whenever Tonya mentions skating, Maja leaves the room or changes the subject. What might happen if Maja continues to handle her jealousy in this way? How might Maja handle her jealousy more positively?

_____

_____

_____

_____

2. Randy shares a room with his brother, Jared. Randy has to get up early to deliver newspapers. He likes to go to sleep at about 10:00 p.m. Jared, on the other hand, likes to stay up past midnight watching the late show. Last night, Randy couldn't get to sleep because of the noise. Instead of asking Jared to turn down the volume, however, Randy yelled, "Jared, you are so thoughtless. I think your brain has turned to mush from watching so much TV." Why might Randy's reaction fail to settle the conflict? How might Randy handle the conflict in a more positive way?

_____

_____

_____

_____

3. Rae and her brother, Don, got into an argument about what kind of party they should have on New Year's Eve. Rae thought a dressy party would be fun. They could serve cheese, crackers, and punch. The girls could wear skirts and the guys could wear sport jackets. Don wanted to have a casual party. Chips and soda would be enough to feed their guests, and everyone could wear jeans. Why is arguing not the most effective way to settle a conflict? How might Rae and Don handle their conflict more positively?

_____

_____

_____

_____

WHEN YOU'RE IN CHARGE

Activity E

Chapter 7

Name _____

Date _____ Period _____

Answer the following questions about caring for younger siblings. If you do not have younger siblings, answer the questions about baby-sitting for young children. Ask a parent to help you answer any questions about which you are uncertain.

1. List the names and ages of any younger siblings living in your home and indicate their genders.

Name	Age	Gender
_____	_____	_____ Male _____ Female
_____	_____	_____ Male _____ Female

2. When do you have to care for these younger siblings? _____
_____

3. What are your responsibilities when caring for younger siblings? _____
_____

4. List two things you should do to help guard the safety of younger siblings in your care.
_____
_____

5. List two activities you can do with younger siblings to amuse them._____
_____
_____

6. Describe a snack you could make for young siblings when you are caring for them._____
_____

7. What discipline problems might you have when caring for younger siblings and how would you handle these problems? _____
_____
_____

8. What rules must you follow regarding visitors, watching television, and taking on the phone when you are caring for younger siblings? _____
_____
_____

9. What should you do if a younger sibling gets injured or becomes sick when you are in charge?
_____

10. Do you enjoy caring for younger siblings? Explain why or why not. _____
_____

SIBLING PYRAMID

Name _____

Date _____ Period _____

Use terms and concepts from the chapter to fill in the pyramid with the words that are missing from the statements.

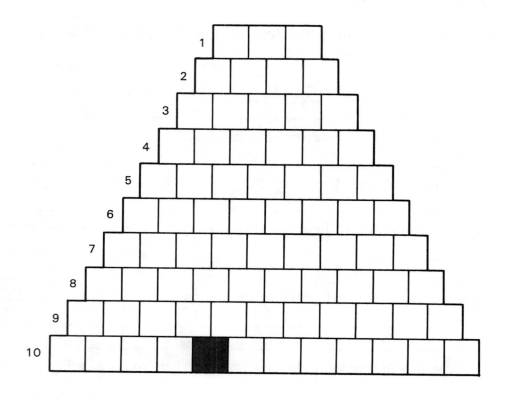

1. Girls tend to imitate their mothers and boys tend to imitate their fathers because of _____ roles.

2. _____ children have no siblings.

3. Identical _____ inherit the same set of characteristics from their parents.

4. The _____, or sex, of children affects the way they relate to their siblings.

5. Competition between siblings is known as sibling _____.

6. People who have the same parents are _____.

7. _____ twins are no more alike than any other two siblings except that they were born on the same day.

8. _____ _____ is a child's place in relation to other children in the family.

9. A stepparent's child from a former marriage is a _____.

10. A _____ _____ is a brother or sister related through only one parent.

COMMUNICATING CLEARLY

―――――――― FEEDBACK ――――――――

Activity A

Chapter 8

Name _____

Date _____ Period _____

Practice your skills as an active listener. Write questions and restated ideas to provide feedback in the following conversation.

"Susan is going to the beach without me."

Feedback: _____

_____

"We were going to go together. Now my mother won't let me go."

Feedback: _____

_____

"I'm not feeling well. My mother thinks I should stay home."

Feedback: _____

_____

"I'm sure I'll feel better next week. Maybe I can go to the beach then."

Feedback: _____

_____

"I don't know if Susan will be able to go to the beach next week."

Feedback: _____

_____

"I think I will ask Richard if he wants to go."

Feedback: _____

_____

"Perhaps both Richard and Susan could go. We could take a picnic lunch and spend the whole day."

Feedback: _____

_____

"I'll have to see if my mother is free to drive us there."

Feedback: _____

_____

ONE- AND TWO-WAY COMMUNICATION

Activity B

Chapter 8

Name _____

Date _____ Period _____

Complete the following communication exercises. Discuss the results in class.

EXERCISE I

1. Use construction paper to make two sets of the following colored shapes: red triangle, yellow triangle, blue square, black circle, white rectangle, green rectangle.
2. Keep one set of shapes for yourself. Give the other set to another student who is sitting in a desk placed back to back with yours.
3. Arrange your shapes into a pattern on top of your desk.
4. Describe this pattern to your partner. HE OR SHE MAY NOT LOOK AT YOUR PATTERN OR ASK YOU ANY QUESTIONS!
5. Based only on your description, your partner must try to form the same pattern you formed.
6. Evaluate this exercise by answering the following questions.

   a. Did your partner arrange his or her shapes correctly? _____

   b. How could you have made your description more clear? _____

   _____

   _____

   c. How could your partner have improved his or her understanding of your description? __

   _____

EXERCISE II

1. Repeat steps 2 and 3 of the exercise above. (You may wish to choose a new partner.)
2. Describe your pattern of shapes to your partner. HE OR SHE MAY NOT LOOK AT YOUR PATTERN!
3. Your partner is free to ask any questions he or she wishes. Based on your description and answers, your partner must try to form the same pattern you formed.
4. Evaluate this exercise by answering the following questions.

   a. Did your partner arrange his or her shapes correctly? _____

   b. Was this exercise easier or harder than the first exercise? _____

   c. How did your partner's ability to ask questions affect his or her success in this exercise?

   _____

   _____

   d. How could communication have been further improved? _____

   _____

   _____

48

COMMUNICATION BLOCKERS

Activity C

Chapter 8

Name _____

Date _____ Period _____

Identify the actions and beliefs that are blocking communication in each of the following situations. Then give suggestions for avoiding the communication blocks.

1. Kayla hit the volleyball out of bounds. That was the third shot she'd missed. Now the game was over and her team had lost.

"Better luck next time, team," said Anna, the team captain. "Let's console ourselves by stopping at Better Burger on the way home."

"Those hamburgers taste like rubber," Kayla replied.

"Well, we don't have to get hamburgers," Anna said. "Their milkshakes are good."

"Their service is too slow," Kayla said. "It will take them half an hour to make milkshakes for all of us."

"We could call our order in before we leave," Anna suggested.

"Better Burger is too far away. If we just want milkshakes, why don't we go to Dairy Frost. It's only two blocks from here," Kayla said.

Anna had turned to another team member. "Let's just go home," she said. "Kayla obviously doesn't want to go out."

What is causing the communication block between Kayla and Anna? _____

_____

_____

How can this block be avoided? _____

_____

_____

2. Tara called Mitch's Bike Shop to check on the repair of her bicycle. "How much damage is there?" she asked.

"It's not bad," Mitch replied.

"Bad! How bad?" Tara wanted to know.

"Really, it shouldn't take long to fix," Mitch said.

"Really bad! My dad is going to be so mad. He'll blame me for leaving my bike in the street where a car could hit it," Tara said.

"Your bike is going to be fine," Mitch tried to reassure her.

"I'll have to pay a fine? You mean leaving your bike in the street is actually against the law?" Tara asked anxiously. "Now I'll be grounded for sure!"

What is causing the communication block between Tara and Mitch? _____

_____

_____

How can this block be avoided? _____

_____

_____

(Continued)

3. Ashley, a new student in Tiffany's health class, uses a wheelchair. Until she met Ashley, the only people Tiffany had ever seen using wheelchairs were sick people in the hospital.

   When Ashley and Tiffany were assigned to do a project together, Ashley suggested they report on muscle disorders. "I already know a lot about them," she said with a smile and a pat of her wheelchair. "We could save some research time."

   "I'd rather do something on bones," Tiffany replied.

   "I have a lot of charts and posters showing bones as well as muscles," Ashley said. "Why don't you come to my house tonight to see if you think we can use them? That would sure be easier than creating new visual aids."

   "I'd rather meet at the library," Tiffany said. "If you're not feeling well enough to leave your house, I'll understand."

What is causing the communication block between Ashley and Tiffany? _____

_____

_____

How can this block be avoided? _____

_____

_____

4. Barry and Charles were walking home from school together. "I can't think of an idea for my English paper," Barry said.

   Charles started dribbling the basketball he was carrying. "You should write about a subject you like. My paper is going to be about Michael Jordan's rise to basketball greatness."

   Barry tried to grab the ball as Charles dribbled. "Have you come up with a topic yet?" he asked.

   Charles blew a large bubble with the gum he was chewing. "Start by jotting down a list of all the things that interest you," he suggested.

   Barry looked in his pocket to see if he had any bubble gum. "I don't even know how to begin to think of a topic," he remarked.

   Charles asked, "Did you notice that new girl in choir? She would be worth writing about! However, if I were you, I'd write about cars. You know more about cars than anyone I know."

   "That girl was really pretty," Barry replied. "But seriously, help me think of a topic for my English paper."

What is causing the communication block between Barry and Charles? _____

_____

_____

How can this block be avoided? _____

_____

_____

COMMUNICATION LEVELS

Activity D

Chapter 8

Name _____

Date _____ Period _____

Fill in the diagram below with photos, pictures from magazines, or drawings to show the kinds of people with whom you interact at each level of communication. Write examples of topics or phrases that would be communicated at each level.

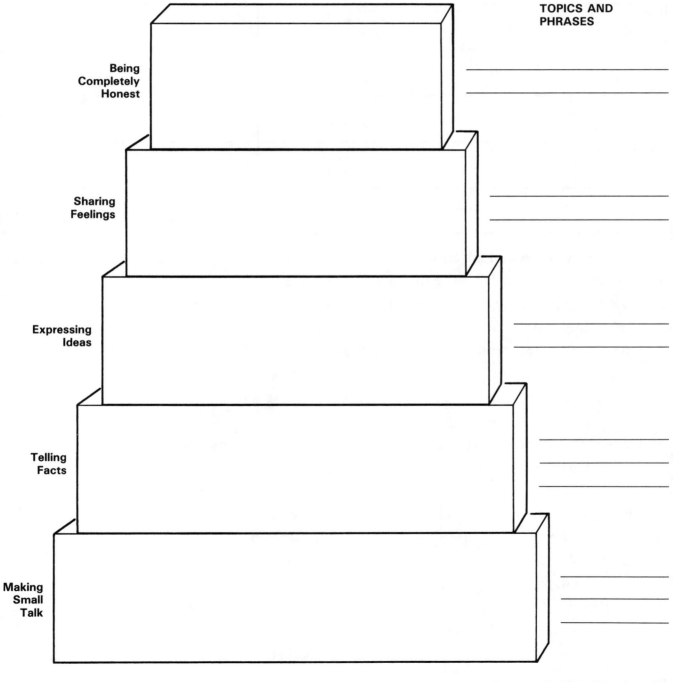

COMMUNICATION DIARY

Activity E

Chapter 8

Name _____

Date _____ Period _____

In the chart below, tally the form of communication you use to send or receive each message communicated in one day. Then answer the following questions and discuss your answers in class.

SENDING		RECEIVING
	Spoken Communication	
	Written Communication	
	Nonverbal Communication	
	Mass Media	
	Art	

1. Which form of communication did you use most often? _____

2. Did you send or receive more messages? _____

3. How were spoken messages communicated? (Check all that apply.)

_____ In person.   _____ On the phone.

4. How were written messages communicated? (Check all that apply.)

_____ Notes/Letters.   _____ Magazines.

_____ Books.   _____ Newspapers.

_____ Homework/Tests.

5. How were nonverbal messages communicated? (Check all that apply.)

_____ Facial expressions.   _____ Gestures.

_____ Posture.   _____ Sounds.

6. Through which forms of mass media did you receive messages? (Check all that apply.)

_____ Radio.   _____ Magazines.

_____ TV.   _____ Billboards/Signs.

_____ Newspapers.   _____ Movies.

7. Through which forms of art did you receive messages? (Check all that apply.)

_____ Paintings/Sculptures.   _____ Music.

_____ Poetry.   _____ Other. _____

COMMUNICATION CHECKLIST

Activity F

Chapter 8

Name _____

Date _____ Period _____

Evaluate your communication skills by responding to each of the following statements according to the way it describes you. Mark "A" for always, "S" for sometimes, and "N" for never. Then score your responses by following the directions below.

Do you:

_____ Try to send constructive messages?

_____ Think about the goal you want to achieve through your communication?

_____ Speak slowly and clearly?

_____ Make your points in a clear order?

_____ Build on your listeners' past knowledge?

_____ Have a good vocabulary?

_____ Avoid using complex words that your listeners may not understand?

_____ Avoid the use of slang?

_____ Try to use the language of the person with whom you are speaking?

_____ Ask a speaker questions when you do not understand what he or she is saying?

_____ Restate a speaker's ideas to be sure that you have understood a message correctly?

_____ Try to reach higher levels of communication with people as you communicate with them more often?

_____ Avoid actions and beliefs that block communication?

_____ Speak to others from the communication zones that will make them feel most comfortable?

_____ Use neat handwriting when communicating through letters and notes?

_____ Write exactly what you mean?

_____ Reread your written communication to catch mistakes?

_____ Use correct grammar and spelling in your written communication?

_____ Use body language to enhance your verbal messages?

_____ Maintain good eye contact when you talk to others?

Give yourself two points for each response marked "A" and one point for each response marked "S." Add up your total points. If you scored 35 or more, you are an excellent communicator; 30-34, you are very good; 25-29, you are good; 24 or less, you better work on it!

_____ "A" responses x 2 =

_____ "S" responses x 1 = + _____

SCORE _____

COMMUNICATION DICTIONARY

Activity G   Name _____

Chapter 8   Date _____ Period _____

Use the letters of the alphabet as clues to help you complete the following statements with terms and concepts from Chapter 8.

1. A_____ _____ involves asking questions and restating ideas.
2. Nonverbal communication is often called B_____ _____.
3. C_____ is a two-part process used to exchange information.
4. D_____ _____ harms relationships.
5. At the third level of communication, people begin to E_____ ideas.
6. Active listeners provide F_____ by asking questions and restating ideas.
7. People who G_____ block communication by complaining.
8. The highest level of communication is one of complete H_____.
9. The I_____ zone is the space within two feet of the body.
10. Strong communication skills are needed by employees to perform many types of J_____.
11. Speakers can communicate effectively by building on their listeners' past K_____.
12. People share their thoughts and feelings to a different degree at each L_____ of communication.
13. M_____ _____ are forms of communication, such as radio, TV, and newspapers, that are used to communicate messages to large numbers of people.
14. N_____ communication involves factors other than words to send messages.
15. To communicate effectively, speakers should state their points in a clear O_____.
16. The P_____ zone is used when the attention of a group is focused on one person.
17. Active listeners can provide feedback by asking Q_____.
18. Good communication is the basis of all strong R_____.
19. S_____ is informal language that is made up of words that do not have standard meanings.
20. Small T_____ is the lowest level of spoken communication.
21. The second step of the communication process takes place when a message is received and U_____.
22. When words are used to send messages, the communication can be described as V_____.
23. People communicate with friends and relatives by W_____ notes and letters.
24. Facial EX_____ are just one type of body language.
25. Some relationships take months or even Y_____ to reach the highest level of communication.
26. Communication Z_____ are four different distances at which people feel comfortable dealing with others.

Chapter 9 FRIENDSHIPS

NEEDS MET BY FRIENDS

Activity A

Chapter 9

Name _____

Date _____ Period _____

Write the name of a different friend in each level of the diagram of human needs shown below. Then give a brief example of how each friend helped fulfill your needs at the level where you've written his or her name.

SELF-ACTUALIZATION

_____ met my
(Friend's name)
needs for self-actualization by

_____

_____

ESTEEM

_____ met my needs for
(Friend's name)
esteem by _____

_____

LOVE AND ACCEPTANCE

_____ met my needs for love and
(Friend's name)
acceptance by _____

_____

SECURITY

_____ met my needs for security by
(Friend's name)

_____

_____

PHYSICAL NEEDS

FORMING FRIENDSHIPS

Activity B

Chapter 9

Name _____

Date _____ Period _____

Analyze the factors that affect your ability to form friendships as you answer the questions below.

1. The number and kinds of friendships you form are related to your chances to meet people. List below the places you go and the groups to which you belong where you might meet friends.

   a. _____

   b. _____

   c. _____

   d. _____

   e. _____

2. Most people have a lot in common with their friends. List below details about your background that you have in common with your friends. (Your list might include interests, hobbies, values, different places where you have lived, etc.)

   a. _____

   b. _____

   c. _____

   d. _____

   e. _____

3. Having a good self-concept helps you form friendships. List below some of the good qualities that you have to offer in a friendship.

   a. _____

   b. _____

   c. _____

   d. _____

   e. _____

4. Knowing how to get along with others is important in making and keeping friends.

   a. What would you do if you got into a disagreement with a friend?

   _____

   _____

   b. How do you show your friends that you care about them?

   _____

   _____

ENDING FRIENDSHIPS

Activity C   Name _____

Chapter 9   Date _____ Period _____

In a small group, discuss the following situations and write your answers to the questions below.

1. Alan and Bob have been good friends for a long time. Lately, tension has been growing between them. They seem to be competing with each other. For instance, when Alan made the soccer team, Bob tried out for the basketball team. Bob bought a new stereo and, within a week, Alan started shopping for a new stereo, too. The other day, Bob saw Alan chatting with Kathy between classes. Three hours later, Bob asked Kathy for a date.

   What might happen if this competition continues? _____

   _____

   How can Alan and Bob relieve the tension in their relationship now? _____

   _____

2. Barbara was jealous when Ms. Goldberg gave Linda the lead in the school play. She started spreading rumors that Linda got the part only because she was one of Ms. Goldberg's "favorites."

   How can spreading rumors affect a friendship? _____

   _____

   How do you think Linda will react when she finds out that Barbara has been spreading rumors?

   _____

3. Ramone discovered that his lockermate, Carl, had been stealing money from the pockets of his jacket. After that, Ramone stopped leaving money in the locker. Although that put an end to the stealing, Ramone felt he could never trust his friend again. Ramone started avoiding Carl. He used the locker only when he knew Carl wouldn't be there. He ignored Carl's greetings when they passed in the hallway. He didn't bother to reply to the party invitation Carl taped to their locker door.

   Why is ignoring Carl a poor way for Ramone to end their friendship? _____

   _____

   What would be a better way for Ramone to end his friendship with Carl? _____

   _____

4. Terri and Jack have been friends since nursery school. They lived next door to each other until last year when Jack moved across town. At first, they called each other often. Lately, Terri has started spending a lot of time with her new boyfriend. Jack has been busy with the student council at his new school.

   What do you think will happen to Jack and Terri's friendship? _____

   _____

   How do you think Jack and Terri feel about this situation? _____

   _____

CONFORMITY

Activity D

Chapter 9

Name _____

Date _____ Period _____

Use the following questions to evaluate your willingness to conform. Check the column that best describes you.

	Yes	No	Maybe
1. Would I watch a TV show I didn't like if my friends wanted to watch it?			
2. If my friends were smoking cigarettes and they offered one to me, would I smoke it?			
3. If my friends were all dancing at a party and I didn't like to dance, would I join them?			
4. If my friends all used swear words, would I use them, too?			
5. Would I wear the latest clothing fad even if I didn't really like it?			
6. If I didn't know how to ski and my friends encouraged me, would I try to learn?			
7. If I knew my friends were all cheating on a test, would I cheat, too?			
8. Would I listen to a radio station I didn't like just because my friends listen to it?			
9. If my friends were serving "spiked" punch at a party, would I drink it?			
10. Would I try a food that sounded unappealing if my friends were all eating it?			
11. If my friends all wanted to ride a roller coaster and I was afraid, would I ride anyway?			
12. If my friends encouraged me to shoplift, would I do it?			
13. If I were new in school, would I try to use local slang phrases to sound like other students?			
14. Would I date someone I didn't really like just because that person was popular?			
15. Would I join a school club with all my friends even if I didn't really have time in my schedule?			

 Chapter 10

THE POPULARITY PUZZLE

——— DEPENDABILITY ———

Activity A

Chapter 10

Name _____

Date _____ Period _____

Fill in the following chart. Identify tasks that various people depend on you to do. Describe the consequences that could result if you fail to do each task. Compare your chart with those of your classmates and discuss.

PEOPLE	TASKS THEY DEPEND ON ME TO DO	CONSEQUENCES IF I FAIL TO DO EACH TASK
Parents		
Siblings		
Friends		
Teachers		
Employers		
Coaches		
Doctors/ Dentists		
Teammates/ Club Members		

OVERCOMING WEAKNESSES

Activity B

Chapter 10

Name _____

Date _____ Period _____

Give suggestions for correcting or overcoming the traits listed below, which some people would consider to be weaknesses. For the last three items, list your weak traits and describe how they might be corrected or overcome.

Traits	Suggestions
1. I can't swim.	_____
	_____
	_____
2. I have a big nose.	_____
	_____
	_____
3. I have a short attention span.	_____
	_____
	_____
4. I'm not a very good speller.	_____
	_____
	_____
5. I'm shy.	_____
	_____
	_____
6. I'm afraid of heights.	_____
	_____
	_____
7. I'm clumsy.	_____
	_____
	_____
8. _____	_____
	_____
9. _____	_____
	_____
10. _____	_____
	_____

OPTIMISTS AND PESSIMISTS

Activity C

Chapter 10

Name _____

Date _____ Period _____

Give examples of optimistic and pessimistic reactions to the following situations.

1. You invite a friend to your home for dinner. You buy all the groceries and start to prepare some of the food. At the last minute, your friend calls and says he can't make it after all.

   As a pessimist, you would:
   say, "Thanks for making me do all this work for nothing." You might wonder why you ever bother to make plans since they never up working out.

   As an optimist, you would:
   _____
   _____
   _____
   _____

2. You plan to spend all day Saturday playing ball in the park with friends. When you wake up Saturday morning, it's pouring rain.

   As a pessimist, you would:
   _____
   _____
   _____
   _____

   As an optimist, you would:
   invite your friends over to play cards, make popcorn, and watch TV. You would say, "I'm sure the weather will be nice enough to play ball tomorrow."

3. You spend the evening writing a report for your history class. Just as you finish, your little sister spills milk all over it.

   As a pessimist, you would:
   _____
   _____
   _____
   _____

   As an optimist, you would:
   _____
   _____
   _____
   _____

4. While reaching for a book on your desk, you knock over a picture of your dog and break the frame.

   As a pessimist, you would:
   _____
   _____
   _____
   _____

   As an optimist, you would:
   _____
   _____
   _____
   _____

FLEXIBILITY

Name _____

Date _____ Period _____

How would a flexible person respond in each of the following situations?

1. Dana and Kristy have been planning for months to go skiing on the second weekend in February. However, this winter has been unusually warm. Now that February is here, there is no snow on the slopes.

    _____

    _____

    _____

2. Monroe had promised his friends that he would drive when they all went to the movies on Friday night. Friday morning, Monroe discovered that he could not get his car started.

    _____

    _____

    _____

3. Carolyn flew to New Orleans to visit her sister. When she arrived, Carolyn learned that the airline had lost all of her luggage.

    _____

    _____

    _____

4. Nadine baked a cake for a birthday party she was giving. An hour before the party, she dropped the cake as she was carrying it to the buffet table.

    _____

    _____

    _____

5. Ron was visiting from out of town to spend a weekend camping with his brother, Tommy. Tommy was counting on borrowing Ron's fishing pole. When Ron arrived, however, he told Tommy that he'd forgotten to bring it.

    _____

    _____

    _____

6. Lemuel and Nathan had tickets for a concert on Saturday night. On Friday, Nathan's mother called to tell Lemuel that Nathan was sick and had to stay in bed all weekend.

    _____

    _____

    _____

POPULARITY CHECKLIST

Activity E

Chapter 10

Name _____

Date _____ Period _____

Check the following statements about popular traits that describe you.

_____ 1. I possess a talent or skill that others admire.

_____ 2. I am intelligent.

_____ 3. I am athletic.

_____ 4. I am attractive.

_____ 5. I am involved in a lot of activities.

_____ 6. I am friendly.

_____ 7. I am outgoing.

_____ 8. I am unselfish.

_____ 9. I am thoughtful.

_____ 10. I am kind.

_____ 11. I am empathetic.

_____ 12. I am honest.

_____ 13. I am dependable.

_____ 14. I am self-confident.

_____ 15. I am willing to try new skills.

_____ 16. I try to correct or overcome my weak points.

_____ 17. I am optimistic.

_____ 18. I am not afraid to fail.

_____ 19. I have a good sense of humor.

_____ 20. I am a leader.

_____ 21. I am a good communicator.

_____ 22. I am tactful.

_____ 23. I am flexible.

_____ 24. I have a good reputation.

_____ 25. I avoid spreading gossip.

What do you think is the most important trait in determining popularity? Explain your answer.

_____

_____

What do you think is the least important trait in determining popularity? Explain your answer.

_____

_____

POPULARITY PUZZLE

Activity F

Chapter 10

Name _____

Date _____ Period _____

Fill in the word puzzle with the characteristics of popular people described below.

1										P								
2										O								
3										P								
4										U								
5										L								
6										A								
7										R								
8					—					I								
9										T								
10										Y								

1. Insight allows _____ people to understand the reasons for a person's feelings or actions.

2. _____ people can look on the bright side of situations that do not work out well.

3. _____ people are popular because others can count on them to do what they say they will do.

4. Popular people use good _____ skills to become more empathetic.

5. _____ people can adapt to new situations.

6. A popular person earns a good _____ by having a number of qualities that others admire.

7. Popular people show their good sense of _____ through their ability to laugh at themselves.

8. _____ people emphasize their strong points and overlook their weak points.

9. _____ people show that they care through little actions as well as special deeds.

10. _____ people are also unselfish.

THE DATING GAME

DATING CROSSWORD

Activity A
Chapter 11

Name _____

Date _____ Period _____

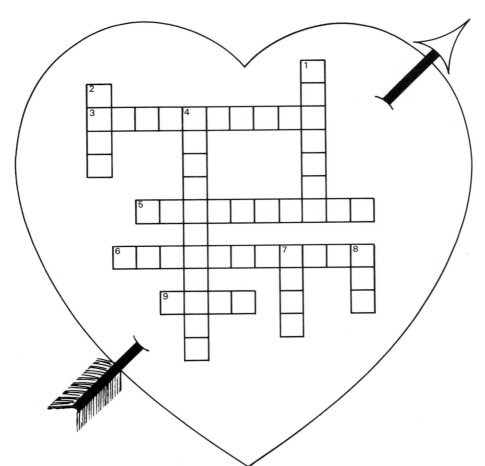

Across

3. Choosing not to have sexual relations is known as _____.
5. Going _____ _____ on a date means that each person pays his or her own way.
6. Beliefs about right and wrong behavior are called _____ _____.
9. _____ is a disease that affects the body's ability to resist infection.

Down

1. Some sexually transmitted diseases can make people _____, or unable to have children.
2. A social meeting between two or more people is called a _____.
4. _____ is an intense feeling of admiration that young teens often have for their first dating partners.
7. _____ is a strong feeling of attachment, warmth, and understanding between two people in more mature dating relationships.
8. An _____ is a disease that is spread through sexual contact.

GROUP DATING OBSERVATION

Activity B

Chapter 11

Name _____

Date _____ Period _____

Observe how teenage men and women interact at a popular local meeting place. Following the observation, respond to the statements and questions below. Use your observation experience as a basis for class discussion.

Location: _____

Approximate average age of young men: _____

Approximate average age of young women: _____

1. Did the teens arrive in couples, single-sex groups, mixed groups, or individually? _____
   _____

2. Did the teens tend to mingle or stay in the groups with which they arrived? _____
   _____

3. Did those who mingled interact with members of the same sex or the opposite sex? _____
   _____

4. Did those who mingled with members of the opposite sex begin to interact immediately or did they wait awhile? _____
   _____

5. Why might some teens want to work into interaction with members of the opposite sex slowly?
   _____
   _____

6. Describe the technique teenage men and women used to interact with each other. (Talking, teasing, pretending to ignore each other, etc.)_____
   _____
   _____

7. From this observation, write your conclusions about group dating. Do you think group dating is a good way to get to know members of the opposite sex? Explain why or why not.
   _____
   _____
   _____
   _____
   _____

A DESIRABLE DATING PARTNER

Activity C

Chapter 11

Name _____

Date _____ Period _____

What traits do you seek in a dating partner? Put a (+) in front of the qualities that are important to you in a dating partner. Put a (−) in front of the qualities that are not important to you in a dating partner. Then answer the questions below.

I want my dating partner:

_____ 1. To compliment me.

_____ 2. To be able to carry on an interesting conversation.

_____ 3. To be polite and use good manners.

_____ 4. To want to spend a lot of time with me.

_____ 5. To be liked by my parents.

_____ 6. To be willing to express his or her feelings.

_____ 7. To place my feelings above his or hers.

_____ 8. To be attractive/handsome.

_____ 9. To be well groomed.

_____ 10. To be about my age.

_____ 11. To have a background similar to mine.

_____ 12. To be a good student.

_____ 13. To be able to spend money on me.

_____ 14. To have a pleasing personality.

_____ 15. To share common interests with me.

_____ 16. To share my values and goals.

_____ 17. To suggest interesting dating activities.

_____ 18. To like my friends.

_____ 19. To avoid trying to change me.

_____ 20. To be honest and sincere.

Of the factors mentioned in the text—physical traits, age, personality, common interests and background, and values and goals—which do you feel is most important in choosing a dating partner?

Explain. _____

_____

How does this factor relate to the above items that you marked as important? _____

_____

_____

PHYSICAL TRAITS

Name _____

Date _____ Period _____

In the space below, mount a magazine picture of a person who has the physical traits of someone you would like to date.

What characteristics do you admire about this person? _____

_____

_____

In a small group, discuss the following question. Write your answer in the space provided.

How important are physical traits compared to the importance of other factors when choosing a dating partner? _____

_____

_____

_____

_____

PLANNING A DATE

Activity E
Chapter 11

Name _____

Date _____ Period _____

Investigate your options for dating activities in your area. Share your findings in class.

1. When should plans for a date be made? _____

2. How would you dress for a date? _____
   _____

3. How much money would you plan to spend on a date? _$_____

4. List area locations and costs for enjoying the following dating activities.

	LOCATION	COST
a. Bowling.	_____	$_____
b. Dancing.	_____	$_____
c. Ice skating.	_____	$_____
d. Movies.	_____	$_____
e. Roller skating.	_____	$_____

5. List other activities you would enjoy on a date.

   _____   _____

   _____   _____

6. List school activities you would enjoy attending with a date.

   _____   _____

   _____   _____

7. List dating activities that you and your partner could enjoy for free.

   _____   _____

   _____   _____

8. List places where you might like to eat while on a date.

   _____   _____

   _____   _____

9. What kind of transportation would you use while on a date?

   _____

10. What time would you plan to begin and end your date?

   _____

ANSWERING DATING QUESTIONS

Activity F

Chapter 11

Name _____

Date _____ Period _____

Complete the following statements to describe your feelings about various dating issues.

1. I could easily become infatuated with someone who...

_____

_____

2. I would know if I were feeling love rather than infatuation by...

_____

_____

3. I would let other people know if I were involved in a steady dating relationship by...

_____

_____

4. I would like to have a steady dating relationship with just one person if...

_____

_____

5. I think the main advantage of being involved in a steady dating relationship is...

_____

_____

6. One thing I don't think I'd like about being involved in a steady dating relationship is...

_____

_____

7. When deciding how to show affection for a dating partner, I would consider...

_____

_____

8. I think a relationship should end when...

_____

_____

9. If my partner wanted to end our relationship and I didn't, I would...

_____

_____

10. If I wanted to stop dating someone, I would...

_____

_____

DATING ADVICE

Name _____

Date _____ Period _____

Pretend you are an advice columnist who writes a "Heartbreak Hotline" column for a local newspaper. Answer the following letters from teens about their dating concerns.

Dear Heartbreak Hotline,
   My boyfriend is two years younger than I am. Is there anything wrong with dating a younger guy? It doesn't bother me, but my friends think it's kind of strange. Why do most girls seem to date older guys?
                              Signed,
                              The Older Woman

Dear Older,

_____

_____

_____

_____

_____

                              Sincerely.
                              H.H.

Dear Heartbreak Hotline,
   Dates are expensive and my part-time job doesn't pay much. How can I keep going out with my girlfriend when my piggy bank is empty?
                              Signed,
                              Bankrupt

Dear Bankrupt,

_____

_____

_____

_____

_____

                              Sincerely,
                              H.H.

Dear Heartbreak Hotline,
   My girlfriend lives with both of her parents. Her father is a doctor and her mother is a college professor. I just live with my mom, who is a checker in a grocery store. How could these differences affect our relationship?
                              Signed,
                              Mr. Opposite

Dear Opposite,

_____

_____

_____

_____

                              Sincerely,
                              H.H.

Dear Heartbreak Hotline,
   I told this really cute guy I'd go to a dance with him next Friday. However, I just found out that I have to visit my grandmother that night. How can I break the date but still let him know that I want to go out with him?
                              Signed,
                              Date Breaker

Dear Breaker,

_____

_____

_____

_____

                              Sincerely,
                              H.H.

(Continued)

Dear Heartbreak Hotline,

I met a wonderful guy! I think I'm in love! I've never felt like this before! My mother says it's just infatuation. How can I know for sure?

Signed,
Starry-eyed

Dear Starry,

_____
_____
_____
_____
_____
_____
_____

Sincerely,
H.H.

Dear Heartbreak Hotline,

My girlfriend and I have been going together for about four months. Lately, I've been feeling that I'm missing out on getting to know other girls. I'm afraid to tell my girlfriend how I feel. How can I break up with her without hurting her feelings?

Signed,
Breakup Blues

Dear Blues,

_____
_____
_____
_____
_____
_____
_____

Sincerely,
H.H.

Dear Heartbreak Hotline,

A guy I've been dating suggested that we stop seeing other people. I really like him, but I'm not sure I want a steady relationship with just one person. Help!

Signed,
Unsteady Dater

Dear Unsteady,

_____
_____
_____
_____
_____
_____
_____

Sincerely,
H.H.

Dear Heartbreak Hotline,

My mom is afraid that I'll go out with the "wrong type" of guys. She asks me a million questions about everyone I want to date. How can I help her stop worrying?

Signed,
Out of Answers

Dear O.O.A.,

_____
_____
_____
_____
_____
_____
_____

Sincerely,
H.H.

PARENTS' CONCERNS

Activity H

Chapter 11

Name _____

Date _____ Period _____

Interview the parent of a teenage child about his or her concerns regarding the child's dating. Then interview a teen about his or her parents' concerns regarding dating. Fill in the responses to the questions below.

Parent Interview

1. What is the gender of your teenage child? _____

2. At what age did you allow your child to begin dating? _____

3. What concerns do you have about your child's dating partners? _____

_____

_____

4. What rules for dating have you set for your child? _____

_____

_____

_____

5. Have dating issues ever been a source of conflict between you and your child? _____

If so, explain the nature of the conflict and how you resolved it. _____

_____

_____

_____

Teen Interview

1. What is your gender? _____

2. At what age did your parents allow you to begin dating? _____

3. What concerns do your parents have about your dating partners? _____

_____

_____

4. What rules for dating have your parents set for you? _____

_____

_____

5. Have dating issues ever been a source of conflict between you and your parents? _____

If so, explain the nature of the conflict and how you resolved it. _____

_____

_____

SEX ON TELEVISION

Activity I

Chapter 11

Name _____

Date _____ Period _____

Watch one-half hour of television on two different days, at two different times, and on two different networks. Complete the following form to describe any references to or depictions of sexual situations in the programs you watch. Compare your findings with those of your classmates and answer the questions at the bottom of the page.

Time: _____ Day: _____

Network: _____ Program: _____

Describe references to or depictions of sexual situations in the program. _____

_____

Describe commercials including references to or depictions of sexual situations.

Product: _____ Description: _____

_____

Product: _____ Description: _____

_____

Time: _____ Day: _____

Network: _____ Program: _____

Describe references to or depictions of sexual situations in the program. _____

_____

Describe commercials including references to or depictions of sexual situations.

Product: _____ Description: _____

_____

Product: _____ Description: _____

_____

1. During what time of day do programs seem to depict more sexual situations? _____

2. What network seems to depict more sexual situations? _____

3. What type(s) of commercials seem to depict more sexual situations? _____

_____

4. How do you feel about the way sexual situations are depicted on television? _____

_____

5. What effect do you think the depiction of sexual situations on television has on the sexual activity of teens? _____

_____

MINDING YOUR MANNERS

A LESSON IN MANNERS

Activity A

Chapter 12

Name _____

Date _____ Period _____

In the following story, Richard has some trouble with his manners at school. Underline all the examples of inappropriate behavior you can find. Then correct the behaviors you underlined as you rewrite the story on a separate sheet of paper.

RUDE RICHARD

When Richard got to his locker after his third period class, he found his lockermate, Derrick, standing there. A pile of books and papers were on the floor at Derrick's feet. "I wish you'd keep your stuff a little neater," Derrick complained. "I can barely fit a notebook in here.

"By the way, you left a tuna sandwich in our locker over the weekend again. My mom's going to be mad when she gets a whiff of my jacket."

Richard just shrugged and said, "You go ahead, I'll take care of the mess on the floor."

After picking up the books and papers, Richard was in a hurry to get to his next class. He slammed his locker door and pushed past students along the left side of the hallway.

Just as Richard reached the wing of the building where his class was located, he saw his friend, Albert. Richard stopped Albert to ask him about going to the game on Friday night. As they were talking, the tardy bell rang. Richard dashed down the hallway and into his classroom.

Richard sat at his desk and opened his notebook. His teacher had started the lesson before he entered the room. Therefore, Richard didn't understand what she was saying. "Could you explain what you just said?" Richard asked. However, he didn't bother to pay attention to her answer. He was busy blowing bubbles with his gum to amuse the girl sitting next to him.

Just before the bell rang, Richard's teacher asked the students to turn in their homework from yesterday. Richard pulled a crumpled paper from his back pocket. There was a jelly stain on it and the handwriting was barely readable. Richard turned in his paper with a smile. He was proud of himself for having gotten it done on time.

The bell rang signaling lunchtime. Richard stuck his gum under his chair and headed for the cafeteria.

When he got to the cafeteria, Richard cut in line behind Albert. They started laughing loudly and poking the girls who were in line in front of them.

After getting his food, Richard sat at a table and started flicking his peas across the room. He nudged the guy beside him. "These hamburgers look like they're made out of dog food," he said. After he finished eating, Richard left his tray and went to the other side of the cafeteria to bother Derrick.

A WELL-MANNERED GUEST

Activity B

Chapter 12

Name _____

Date _____ Period _____

For each of the following questions, select the best answer and write the letter in the blank.

_____ 1. You should treat your host's property _____ you treat your own.
a. The same as.
b. Better than.

_____ 2. In someone else's home, you should _____ propping your feet up on the coffee table.
a. Make yourself comfortable by.
b. Avoid.

_____ 3. _____ ask your host for permission before doing things you would do at home.
a. You should.
b. You do not need to.

_____ 4. You would be _____ your bounds if you opened your host's refrigerator to fix yourself a snack.
a. Overstepping.
b. Within.

_____ 5. Avoid rough play _____.
a. Indoors.
b. Outdoors.

_____ 6. Your host _____ have to spend a lot of time cleaning after your visit.
a. Should.
b. Should not.

_____ 7. _____ should hang up wet towels when you are doing using them.
a. Your host.
b. You.

_____ 8. Being _____ is part of the good manners you should follow as a guest.
a. On time.
b. "Fashionably" late.

_____ 9. You should _____ before a meal.
a. Relax in the living room.
b. Offer to help.

_____ 10. Well-mannered quests _____ plans for entertainment.
a. Make their own.
b. Agree to follow their hosts'.

ETIQUETTE EXPERT

Activity C

Chapter 12

Name _____

Date _____ Period _____

Pretend you write a column for a local newspaper called "The Etiquette Expert." Answer the following letters from readers who have questions about table manners when eating out.

Dear Etiquette Expert,
Whenever we go out to eat, my mother scolds me for putting my purse on the table. Why is this considered to be bad manners?
Signed,
Handbag Hassles

Dear Hassles,

_____

_____

_____

_____

_____

_____

Sincerely,
E.E.

Dear Etiquette Expert,
I always feel nervous when I go to a fancy restaurant. I never know which fork to use. Are there some guidelines I should follow?
Signed,
Confused

Dear Confused,

_____

_____

_____

_____

_____

_____

Sincerely,
E.E.

Dear Etiquette Expert,
I never know how much money I should leave for a waiter at a restaurant. What is the proper procedure for tipping?
Signed,
Timid Tipper

Dear Timid,

_____

_____

_____

_____

_____

_____

Sincerely,
E.E.

Dear Etiquette Expert,
I saw a restaurant scene in a movie where the waiter brought the bill on a small tray. Could you explain the meaning of this?
Signed,
Puzzled About Payment

Dear Puzzled,

_____

_____

_____

_____

_____

_____

Sincerely,
E.E.

TELEPHONE TIPS

Activity D

Chapter 12

Name _____

Date _____ Period _____

In the following puzzle, the numbers below the blanks represent letters on a telephone dial. Use the clues and the numbers to fill in the blanks.

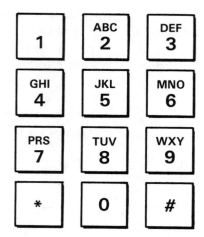

1. Make calls during ___ ___ ___ and ___ ___ ___ ___ ___ ___ ___ hours.
   3 2 9   3 8 3 6 4 6 4

2. Speak directly into the ___ ___ ___ ___ ___ ___ ___ ___ ___ .
   6 6 8 8 4 7 4 3 2 3

3. Speak in a ___ ___ ___ ___ ___ voice.
   2 5 3 2 7

4. Keep your mouth ___ ___ ___ ___ ___ so your listener can understand you.
   3 6 7 8 9

5. Keep your conversations ___ ___ ___ ___ ___ when someone is expecting a call.
   7 4 6 7 8

6. Avoid talking about ___ ___ ___ ___ ___ ___ ___ ___ ___ ___ ___
   3 6 2 2 7 7 2 7 7 4 6 4

   subjects when others are in the room.

7. Following some safety measures can help you avoid trouble with ___ ___ ___ ___ ___
   7 7 2 6 5

   ___ ___ ___ ___ ___ ___ ___ .
   2 2 5 5 3 7 7

8. Avoid giving your ___ ___ ___ ___ or ___ ___ ___ ___ ___
   6 2 6 3   7 4 6 6 3

   ___ ___ ___ ___ ___ ___ until you know who is calling.
   6 8 6 2 3 7

9. Do not say that you are ___ ___ ___ ___ ___ ___ ___ ___ ___ .
   4 6 6 3 2 5 6 6 3

10. You need to respond when a caller speaks to you because he or she cannot see your

   ___ ___ ___ ___ ___ ___ ___ ___ ___ ___ ___ ___ .
   2 6 3 9 5 2 6 4 8 2 4 3

Chapter 13

BEING A SMART CONSUMER

——— SHORT- AND LONG-TERM GOALS ———

Activity A

Chapter 13

Name _____

Date _____ Period _____

Put an "S" in the blank beside each short-term goal. Put an "L" in the blank beside each long-term goal. Then complete the diagram at the bottom of the page.

_____ 1. Buying a car.

_____ 2. Becoming a supervisor in a company.

_____ 3. Passing a math test.

_____ 4. Buying a home.

_____ 5. Going to see a movie.

_____ 6. Doing the laundry.

_____ 7. Taking a trip around the world.

_____ 8. Getting a date for a party next weekend.

_____ 9. Eating lunch.

_____ 10. Buying a new shirt.

_____ 11. Having children.

_____ 12. Getting married.

_____ 13. Fixing a flat bicycle tire.

_____ 14. Graduating from college.

_____ 15. Writing a book.

_____ 16. Writing a history report.

In the illustration below, label the right side of the riverbank with one of your long-term goals. Then label the stepping stones with three short-term goals that will help you reach the long-term goal.

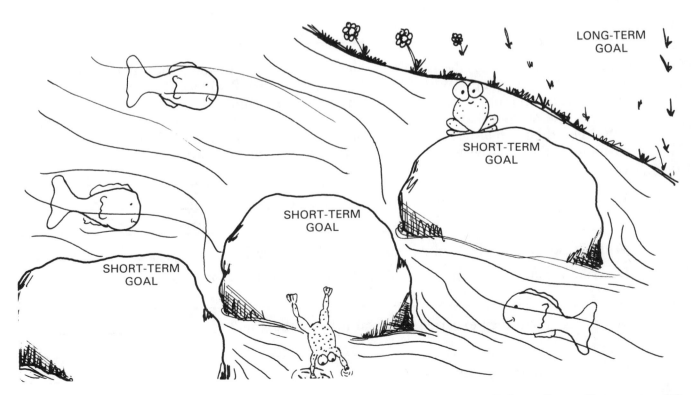

USING THE MANAGEMENT PROCESS

In a small group, discuss how the teens in each of the following situations could use the management process to achieve goals. Write your responses in the space provided.

1. Jared has studied Spanish for the last three years. During this time, he has developed a good relationship with his Spanish teacher, Mr. Ruiz. If it hadn't been for Mr. Ruiz, Jared might never have started writing to Miguel, a pen pal in Spain.

   Mr. Ruiz also helped Jared get a job at a local bookstore. Jared's job allows him to earn extra money. It also gives him a chance to read travel books. He hopes to visit Spain someday.

   a. What is Jared's goal? _____

   b. What resources does Jared have available? _____

   _____

   c. Which resources might Jared use to reach his goal? _____

   d. Describe a plan of action Jared might follow to reach his goal. _____

   _____

   e. What might Jared experience as he follows the plan? _____

   _____

   f. How might Jared evaluate the plan? _____

   _____

2. Whitney loves the water. She is on the school swim team. In fact, she came in first in last year's state championships. Whitney works as a lifeguard at the local pool. When she's not working, she's often at the marina watching boats or fishing.

   It was at the marina that Whitney met Darrell. Darrell goes to college in Florida. Darrell told Whitney about a marine biology program at his school. Whitney thinks the program sounds tailor-made for her. However, she knows her parents can't afford to pay for college.

   a. What is Whitney's goal? _____

   b. What resources does Whitney have available? _____

   _____

   c. Which resources might Whitney use to reach her goal? _____

   d. Describe a plan of action Whitney might follow to reach her goal. _____

   _____

   e. What might Whitney experience as she follows the plan? _____

   _____

   f. How might Whitney evaluate the plan? _____

   _____

THE INFLUENCE OF ADVERTISING

Activity C

Chapter 13

Name _____

Date _____ Period _____

In the space below, mount an ad from a magazine or newspaper. Then answer the questions at the bottom of the page.

1. What type of advertising appeal is being used in this ad? _____

   Describe how the appeal is being used. _____

   _____

2. Would this ad convince you to purchase this product? _____

   Explain why or why not. _____

   _____

USING CONSUMER INFORMATION

Name _____

Date _____ Period _____

Complete the form below as you use a consumer resource from the library to research a product of your choice.

1. Type of product you are researching: _____

2. Consumer resource you used to conduct your research: _____

3. What brands were compared in the report you read?

   _____   _____

   _____   _____

   _____   _____

   _____   _____

4. What was the price range of the brands being compared? _____

5. What types of features were found on the brands being compared? _____

   _____

6. Briefly describe three tests that were performed on the products. Name the brand that was rated highest for each test.

   a. Test: _____

   _____

   Brand rated highest: _____

   b. Test: _____

   _____

   Brand rated highest: _____

   c. Test: _____

   Brand rated highest: _____

7. Which brand was rated best overall? _____

8. How much would you be willing to spend if you were buying this product? _____

9. What features would be most important to you if you were buying this product? _____

   _____

10. How would you use the information in this report when making a purchase decision?

   _____

   _____

DEVELOP A BUDGET

Activity E

Chapter 13

Name _____

Date _____ Period _____

Complete the form to develop a budget based on your own income and expenses for one month. List the sources of income and the types of fixed and flexible expenses. Estimate the dollar amount for each item listed. Then total your estimated income and your estimated expenses. Compare the two figures and answer the questions that follow.

Income:

_____ $ _____

_____ $ _____

_____ $ _____

Total income $ _____

Fixed expenses:

_____ $ _____

_____ $ _____

_____ $ _____

Flexible expenses:

_____ $ _____

_____ $ _____

_____ $ _____

Total expenses $ _____

1. Is your income equal to your expenses? _____

2. If your income were greater than your expenses, what would you do with the extra money?

   _____

   _____

3. If your income were less than your expenses, how could you increase your income? _____

   _____

4. How could you reduce your expenses? _____

   _____

5. What are your savings goals? _____

   _____

6. How can using a budget help you meet your goals? _____

   _____

Activity F
Chapter 13

Name _____

Date _____ Period _____

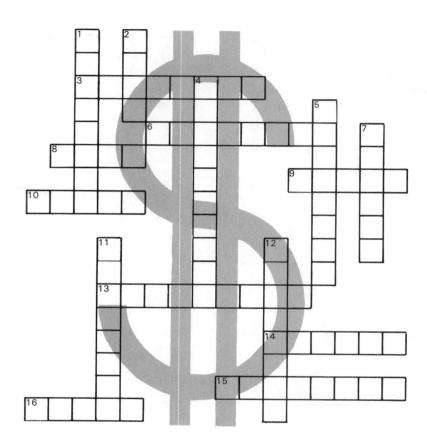

Across

3. Material items are _____ resources.
6. Someone who uses goods and services is known as a _____.
8. Being in _____ means owing someone money.
9. Consumer products are known as _____.
10. _____ resources are resources that come from within people.
13. A _____ goal can be achieved in a few days or weeks.
14. Money a person receives is called _____.
15. A _____ expense does not occur regularly or varies in amount from one month to the next.
16. A _____ expense has to be paid regularly.

Down

1. A goal that may take months, years, or even a whole lifetime to achieve is called a _____ goal.
2. An item that is desired but is not needed to live is a _____.
4. Carefully using available means to reach goals is known as _____.
5. A _____ is a rank of how important something is to a person.
7. A plan for using money is called a _____.
11. A _____ is a means used to reach goals.
12. Tasks that have value to consumers are called _____.

Chapter 14

MANAGING YOUR TIME

—————— YOUR DAILY TIME PLAN ——————

Activity A

Chapter 14

Name _____

Date _____ Period _____

Complete the daily time plan to show how you plan to use your time tomorrow. Begin by listing your high priority tasks. These should include sleeping, eating, going to school, and studying as well as any scheduled meetings you have to attend. Then fill in lower priority tasks, such as visiting friends or working on hobbies. Complete the "to do" list on the next page with any little tasks you will have to do. Indicate where in your daily time plan you will do the tasks on this list. Don't forget to keep some time open in your plan for flexibility. Follow the plan tomorrow and then answer the questions at the end of the next page.

A.M.	P.M.
12:00 midnight	12:00 noon
12:30	12:30
1:00	1:00
1:30	1:30
2:00	2:00
2:30	2:30
3:00	3:00
3:30	3:30
4:00	4:00
4:30	4:30
5:00	5:00
5:30	5:30
6:00	6:00
6:30	6:30
7:00	7:00
7:30	7:30
8:00	8:00
8:30	8:30
9:00	9:00
9:30	9:30
10:00	10:00
10:30	10:30
11:00	11:00
11:30	11:30

(Continued)

To Do List

(Number listed items from most to least important.)

Phone calls:

Chores:

Errands:

1. Were you able to stick to your time plan throughout the day? _____

   If not, at what point did you stray from the plan? _____

   _____

   What caused you to stray from the plan? _____

   _____

   _____

2. What tasks, if any, took more time than you had planned? _____

   _____

3. What tasks, if any, took less time than you had planned? _____

   _____

4. Did the plan help you make better use of your time? _____

   Explain why or why not. _____

   _____

   _____

5. What changes would you make to the plan before following it again? _____

   _____

   _____

TIME WASTERS

Activity B

Chapter 14

Name _____

Date _____ Period _____

Identify the time-wasting problem in each of the following situations. Then suggest ways the problem could be avoided.

1. Cecil's science project is due in three days, and he hasn't even started it yet! He's known about the project for months, but it seemed so big, he didn't know where to start.

   The assignment was to conduct research, design an experiment, and write a report. However, the research was supposed to involve at least 10 references. The experiment was supposed to be tested and revised twice. The report had to be at least 15 pages long.

   Now Cecil is in a panic. He knows there is no way he can complete the project in three days. If he doesn't turn in a project, he'll fail the class.

   a. What is Cecil's time-wasting problem? _____

   b. How might Cecil have avoided this problem when he was first given the assignment?

   _____

   _____

   _____

2. Rita wanted to make a cake as a surprise for her sister. She got out the mixer. Then she got out the flour and a measuring cup.

   Rita realized she didn't even know what kind of cake she was going to make. She remembered seeing a recipe in a magazine that sounded good. She went to look it up. She paged through all the magazines in the living room. Finally, she found the right magazine in her bedroom.

   Once she was back in the kitchen, Rita got out the eggs and a mixing bowl. She measured the flour into the bowl, and then got out the sugar. She discovered that the rubber spatula was dirty, so she stopped to wash it. Next, Rita checked the recipe and noticed that it called for cocoa. Rita couldn't find any cocoa in the cupboard, so she made a trip to the store. After returning from the store, Rita didn't have enough time to finish the cake before her sister came home.

   a. What is Rita's time-wasting problem? _____

   b. How might Rita have avoided this problem when she first decided to bake a cake?

   _____

   _____

   _____

(Continued)

3. Benny wants everything he does to be perfect. For instance, last month Benny was organizing his baseball cards in an album. As he placed each card in the album, he carefully cataloged it in a notebook. He was just about done when he discovered that he had overlooked a card. It belonged on the second page of the album. Benny went back through the album and moved each card one slot forward to make room for the extra card. Then he completely rewrote his notebook entries so everything would be in order.

   a. What is Benny's time-wasting problem? _____

   b. How could Benny use his time more effectively? _____

   _____

4. Yesterday morning when Sally's alarm went off, she rolled over and slept for a few more minutes. Then she got up and got dressed. She dashed out the door, claiming that she didn't have time to eat breakfast. She got to the bus stop ten minutes early. Sally talked to her friends until the bus came.

   When she got to school, Sally chatted with other friends until the bell rang. Sally's first class was math. Sally pulled out her homework and remembered that she hadn't solved the last two equations. She had to turn in the assignment incomplete. Next, Sally had English class. Five minutes before the end of class, the teacher assigned a one-page essay to be written for class tomorrow. Sally didn't have an idea for an essay topic. Instead of starting the assignment, she wrote a note to a friend.

   a. What is Sally's time-wasting problem? _____

   b. How could Sally use her time more effectively? _____

   _____

5. Gary is always on the go. He is on the student council. He is a member of the marching band. He is in the youth choir at church. He is in a scout troop. He has a paper route. He even volunteers at the animal shelter once a week.

   Gary's schedule keeps him so busy that he frequently misses meals. He often stays up until 1:00 in the morning to get his homework done. He never has time to get together with his friends, either.

   Although Gary is involved in a lot of activities, he doesn't always do them well. At last week's student council meeting, Gary spent the whole time yawning and staring into space. He didn't have the energy to complete the drills at band practice on Thursday. A sore throat that kept him from singing with the youth choir on Sunday has now progressed into an infection. He's been too sick to deliver papers or go to the animal shelter for the last three days. He'll have to miss the scout camping trip this weekend, too.

   a. What is Gary's time-wasting problem? _____

   b. How could Gary use his time more effectively? _____

   _____

   _____

HOUSEHOLD CHORES GAME

Activity C

Chapter 14

Name _____

Date _____ Period _____

Evaluate your time management skills for doing household chores by playing the game below with two or three of your classmates. Use buttons or circles of paper for markers. Take turns flipping a coin to move around the board. If the coin is flipped "heads," move the marker two spaces. If the coin is flipped "tails," move the marker one space. The player who finishes first is the winner.

1. **START**	2. Cleaning the bathroom, the least popular chore, is rotated among family members from week to week. Move ahead 1 space.	3. 	4. You didn't gather all of your cleaning supplies before beginning to wash windows. Move back 1 space.
8. 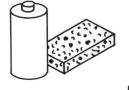	7. You failed to wash the dishes last night, so your father had to do them for you. Go back to start.	6.	5. You dovetailed breakfast preparation tasks by mixing up a pitcher of orange juice while waiting for the toast to pop up. Take another turn.
9. You avoided getting out the vacuum cleaner twice by vacuuming the hallway at the same time you were vacuuming your bedroom. Move ahead 2 spaces.	18. Everyone in the family keeps running out of clean socks and underwear. Miss a turn while you decide how often the laundry needs to be done.	17.	16. You agreed to cook dinner while giving your five-year-old brother the task of setting the table. Move ahead 1 space.
10. No one in the family is taking responsibility for any of the household chores. Miss a turn while you decide how to divide tasks among family members.	19.	20. **FINISH** Congratulations! You've learned to use your time effectively to complete your household chores.	15. Cleaning the oven is the hardest job in the kitchen. You saved it for last, and now you're too tired to do it. Move back to space 10.
11.	12. You used a rag instead of a mop to wash the kitchen floor. Move back 1 space.	13. You agreed to take over your brother's chores while he is busy rehearsing for the class play. Take another turn.	14. 

STUDY HABITS SURVEY

Activity D

Chapter 14

Name _____

Date _____ Period _____

Survey five students about their study habits. Record their answers in the chart provided. Compile your results with those of your classmates. Write an article for your school paper reporting your findings.

1. What is your gender?   a. Male.   b. Female.

2. What is your grade level? _____

3. How much time do you spend studying and doing homework each day?   a. Less than 1 hour.   b. 1-2 hours.   c. 2-3 hours.   d. More than 3 hours.

4. Which subject do you study most? _____

5. Which subject do you study least? _____

6. What time of day do you usually study?   a. Before school.   b. After school.   c. In the evening.

7. Where do you study?   a. At home.   b. In the library.   c. Other: _____

8. Do you do homework during study halls at school?   a. Yes.   b. No.

9. Do you start preparing for major tests and big projects well in advance?   a. Yes.   b. No.

10. Do you feel your study habits could be improved?   a. Yes.   b. No.

SURVEY RESPONSES

QUESTION	PERSON 1	PERSON 2	PERSON 3	PERSON 4	PERSON 5
1.					
2.					
3.					
4.					
5.					
6.					
7.					
8.					
9.					
10.					

LEISURE INTERESTS INVENTORY

Activity E

Chapter 14

Name _____

Date _____ Period _____

Answer the following questions to help you define how you like to spend your leisure time.

1. How much leisure time do you have each week?_____

2. How much money can you afford to spend each week on leisure activities? $_____

3. What is a club in which you're a member or would like to become a member? _____
   _____

4. What is a class, other than a school class, that you've taken or would like to take? _____
   _____

5. What is a game that you enjoy playing? _____

6. What is a TV show that you like? _____

   When is it on? _____

7. What kinds of activities do you enjoy doing with a group of friends?_____
   _____

8. What kinds of activities do you enjoy doing by yourself? _____
   _____

9. What artistic hobbies do you have? _____

10. What crafts do you enjoy? _____

11. What kinds of items do you collect? _____

12. What individual sports do you enjoy?_____

13. What team sports do you enjoy? _____

14. Check all of the following types of entertainment that you enjoy.

   _____ Plays. _____ Lectures. _____ Concerts.

   _____ Fairs. _____ Circuses. _____ Movies.

15. Do you like to sing? _____

16. Do you play a musical instrument?_____

   If so, which one? _____

17. What kind of music do you like? _____

18. Where would you most like to go on a vacation? _____

   Why would you like to go there? _____
   _____

19. Who would you like to travel with on a vacation trip? _____

20. For what kinds of occasions do you like to give or attend parties? _____
   _____

TIME CHART

Name _____

Date _____ Period _____

Complete each chart and answer the question that follows.

Total Time

Divide the circle below to form a pie chart. Show how your time is divided between home, school, other activities, and leisure time.

If you had total control over how you spent your time, how would you like the segments in this chart to change? _____

_____

Time at Home

Divide the circle below to form a pie chart. Show how your time at home is divided between family and chores.

If you had total control over how you spent your time, how would you like the segments in this chart to change? _____

_____

Time for School

Divide the circle below to form a pie chart. Show how your time for school is divided between class time, study time, and school activities.

If you had total control over how you spent your time, how would you like the segments in this chart to change? _____

_____

Chapter 15

LOOKING GOOD

GROOMING AIDS

Activity A

Chapter 15

Name _____

Date _____ Period _____

In the chart below, list all the grooming aids you use to help you care for various parts of your body.

	PRODUCT
Body	
Face	
Hair Removal	
Feet	

	PRODUCT
Hair	
Teeth	
Hands	

WARDROBE INVENTORY

Activity B

Chapter 15

Name _____

Date _____ Period _____

In the chart below, list your activities and the clothes needed for each one.

               Activities   Clothing needs

1. _____   _____

2. _____   _____

3. _____   _____

4. _____   _____

5. _____   _____

Use the following chart to describe the color, fabric, and condition of each item in your wardrobe.

Item	Keep	Repair	Discard

Do the items in your wardrobe meet your clothing needs?_____

How can your inventory help you plan clothing purchases? _____

_____

Activity C

Chapter 15

Name _____

Date _____ Period _____

In the following puzzle, the numbers below the blanks represent letters on a telephone dial. Use the clues and the numbers to fill in the blanks with the correct answers.

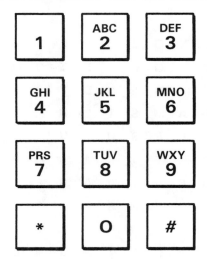

1. Socks and undergarments should be changed daily to prevent odors and growth of

   ___ ___ ___ ___ ___ ___ ___ ___.
    2   2   2   8   3   7   4   2

2. Before laundering, treat any ___ ___ ___ ___ ___ ___.
                                  7   8   2   4   6   7

3. Check ___ ___ ___ ___ ___ ___ ___ ___ ___ ___ for any special washing
          2   2   7   3   5   2   2   3   5   7
   instructions.

4. Sort clothes according to ___ ___ ___ ___ ___ and ___ ___ ___ ___ ___
                              2   6   5   6   7   9   2   8   3   7

   ___ ___ ___ ___ ___ ___ ___ ___ ___ ___.
    8   3   6   7   3   7   2   8   8   7   3

5. White items can be washed in ___ ___ ___ water.
                                  4   6   8

6. Use warm water for light colors and ___ ___ ___ ___ ___ ___ ___ ___ ___
                                         7   3   7   6   2   6   3   6   8

   ___ ___ ___ ___ ___ items.
    7   7   3   7   7

7. Using cold water will help keep dark colors from ___ ___ ___ ___ ___ ___.
                                                      3   2   3   4   6   4

8. After washing, clothes may be dried in an automatic dryer or on a

   ___ ___ ___ ___ ___ ___ ___ ___ ___ ___ ___.
    2   5   6   8   4   3   7   5   4   6   3

9. Fold or hang clothes to prevent ___ ___ ___ ___ ___ ___ ___ ___.
                                    9   7   4   6   5   5   3   7

10. Clothes made of wool, silk, and acetate usually should be

    ___ ___ ___ - ___ ___ ___ ___ ___ ___ ___.
     3   7   9   2   5   3   2   6   3   3

Activity D

Chapter 15

Name _____

Date _____ Period _____

Read the definitions and write the corresponding terms in the blanks. Then find the terms in the word maze and circle them. (Terms are located forward, backward, horizontally, vertically, and diagonally in the maze.)

```
N E U N I T O K O Z D P L K P I A O P F U
D E R M A T O L O G I S T O M Q L U N Q A
C F K U E C H Z B E S D Y P S B I T M R I
I E R U C I N A M S T Z U X E D A G Q G Y
M H G O R I E E E S U L V T L L N W F S B
J F D N G W D L T M S W N C C M G Z A C N
E T Q S E H A E R E A A B F I E N Q D O E
J E O T N A R I P S R E P I T N A R I W O
G U R A D U L E V O K G S I U V H T T L N
Y Q P I T O G N D L T M J R C T A I Y I T
H A H S G R O O M I N G H O T R Z J K C F
F L O J O P E Q M C L O S R I U F L O K F
K P K N L D U R X E K X X P W R N E M D U
L I O M A D I N E N O T S E C I M U P L R
E M J R L E D G T U V R Q X Y W P K R S D
K P E I E H O W E W E M E H I Q N A V D N
Z L N O I S S E R P M I T S R I F V T U A
G E C M F B J C Y O C B Z C L Z E F A J D
D S L B P C O M P A R I S O N D B S V Y T
```

1. A product that interferes with the growth of bacteria and thus controls body odor.

1. _____

2. What people think of someone when they first meet that person. (Two words.)

2. _____

3. A treatment to care for hands and fingernails.

3. _____

4. Small sores that usually appear on the face, neck, and back caused from skin oil trapped inside pores.

4. _____

5. The position of the body while standing, sitting, and walking.

5. _____

6. A bad case of pimples on the skin.

6. _____

(Continued)

7. Thin, dry scales that form on the scalp.

7. _____

8. Buying an item that suddenly appeals to the shopper is known as _____ buying.

8. _____

9. Tiny openings in the skin.

9. _____

10. Little ridges of skin that form at the base of fingernails and toenails.

10. _____

11. A doctor who specializes in the care and treatment of skin conditions.

11. _____

12. Tiny insects that can live in human hair and cause severe itching.

12. _____

13. A film that forms on teeth and can cause tooth decay.

13. _____

14. A product that controls body odor and wetness due to perspiration.

14. _____

15. Cleaning and caring for the body.

15. _____

16. A treatment to care for feet and toenails.

16. _____

17. Sweat.

17. _____

18. A patch of hair that grows in a different direction than the rest of the hair.

18. _____

19. A bit of skin that comes loose at the corners of fingernails.

19. _____

20. A rough stone that can be used to remove dead skin from the feet. (Two words.)

20. _____

21. Comparing similar items before buying them is called _____ shopping.

21. _____

22. A short-lived clothing trend.

22. _____

23. A line of stitches that holds two pieces of fabric together.

23. _____

24. The turned-up edge at the bottom of a garment.

24. _____

PERSONAL CARE SCHEDULE

Activity E

Chapter 15

Name _____

Date _____ Period _____

Complete the chart below to indicate how often you should do each of the following tasks to keep yourself well groomed.

TASK	DAILY	WEEKLY	OTHER
Shower/Bathe			
Wash face			
Brush teeth			
Floss teeth			
Comb/Brush hair			
Shave			
Shampoo			
Haircut			
Dental checkup			
Manicure			
Pedicure			
Do laundry			
Wardrobe inventory			
Buy new clothes			
Repair clothes			
Other:_____			
Other:_____			
Other:_____			

Think about your present grooming habits. List below two goals for improvement:

1. _____

_____

2. _____

_____

TAKING CARE OF YOURSELF

──── DAILY FOOD GUIDE ────

Activity A   Name _____

Chapter 16   Date _____ Period _____

Clip magazine pictures of foods in each group of the Daily Food Guide and mount them in the spaces below. Fill in the blanks to show how many servings you should have from each group each day. Then answer the questions that follow.

MEAT AND MEAT ALTERNATES GROUP	MILK AND MILK PRODUCTS GROUP
I need at least ____ servings from this group each day.	I need at least ____ servings from this group each day.
FRUITS AND VEGETABLES GROUP	**BREAD AND CEREAL GROUP**
I need at least ____ servings from this group each day.	I need at least ____ servings from this group each day.

1. Define diet. _____

2. Define nutrient. _____

3. Give three examples of foods in the fats and sweets group.

     a. _____ b. _____ c. _____

4. Give two reason why you should limit the amounts of fats and sweets you eat.

     a. _____

     b. _____

DE-STRESSING SITUATIONS

Activity B

Chapter 16

Name _____

Date _____ Period _____

Identify the source of stress for the teenagers in each of the following situations. Then suggest a way that the teen might relieve or avoid the stress he or she is feeling.

1. Lately, Rhonda has been getting stomachaches in her first period history class. Rhonda has never liked history. The fact that she doesn't get along with her teacher only makes matters worse.

   In the last few weeks, Rhonda has been putting off doing her history homework in the evenings. Instead, she's been getting up early and doing it before school. This often causes Rhonda to be rushed in the mornings. Sometimes she doesn't get her homework finished. Other times, she is late for school.

   What do you think is causing Rhonda's stomachaches? _____

   _____

   _____

   _____

   _____

   How do you think Rhonda can avoid getting stomachaches? _____

   _____

   _____

   _____

2. Josh often has trouble getting to sleep at night. He lies awake worrying. He worries about his health. He worries about his grades. He worries about his future. He worries about dates. He worries about money. He also worries about not being able to sleep!

   What do you think is causing Josh's sleeplessness? _____

   _____

   _____

   _____

   _____

   What do you think might help Josh rest easier? _____

   _____

   _____

   _____

   _____

(Continued)

3. Lately, Renee has felt irritable, but she can't understand why she feels this way. She doesn't have a hectic schedule or a lot of worries. In fact, all Renee ever does is sit in front of the TV and eat junk food.

   Renee's evenings are all about the same. When she gets home from school, she plops in front of the TV to watch reruns. She sits there eating chips and drinking soda until the six o'clock news. Then she switches to early evening game shows and cookies. Renee munches on popcorn during her favorite nighttime shows and nibbles on candy during the late movie.

   What do you think is causing Renee's irritability? _____

   _____

   How do you think Renee can relieve her irritability? _____

   _____

4. Kevin is an active guy. Lately, his busy schedule has been interrupted by headaches. Normally, Kevin jogs two miles every morning. Then he comes home, showers, and goes to school. As eighth grade class president, Kevin often spends his lunch period arranging meetings. He also has to write letters, post notices, and type memos. After school, Kevin has band practice. Then he heads to work where he spends a couple of hours helping at his father's store. After work, Kevin stops at home for a quick dinner. Then he goes to visit his girlfriend for an hour or two. He returns home and does his homework before going to bed.

   What do you think is causing Kevin's headaches? _____

   _____

   How do you think Kevin can avoid getting headaches? _____

   _____

5. Matthew feels he has no control over his life. This feeling has caused him to become depressed. He hasn't always felt this way. A few months ago, Matthew's father got a new job. This meant that Matthew and his family had to move to a new town. The week before the move, Matthew's grandmother died.

   Matthew has been in his new home for two months now. However, his life still hasn't gotten back to "normal." Last week, Matthew's mother had a baby girl. His parents brought her home from the hospital yesterday.

   What do you think is causing Matthew's depression? _____

   _____

   How do you think Matthew can overcome his depression? _____

   _____

HEALTH RISKS CROSSWORD

Activity C

Chapter 16

Name _____

Date _____ Period _____

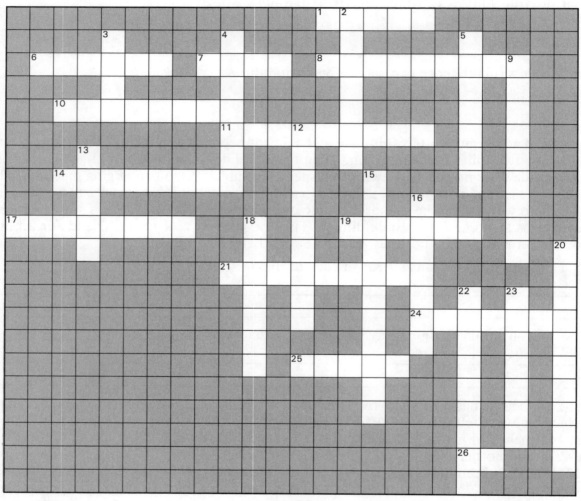

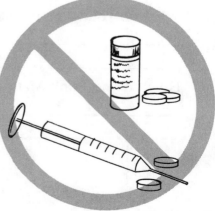

(Continued)

Across

1. Alcohol can cause damage to the brain, heart, and _____.
6. People who smoke are more likely to get lung diseases, including lung _____.
7. Selling drugs may result in the punishment of a _____ sentence.
8. Alcoholics and heavy drinkers may suffer from memory losses called _____.
10. _____ are harmful drugs taken illegally by some people involved in sports to build strength.
11. Sniffing the fumes of _____, such as glue and fabric protectors, can cause damage to the kidneys and blood.
14. Teens must learn to resist peer _____ to use tobacco, alcohol, and other drugs.
17. Cigarette smoking can _____ teeth.
19. Smoking marijuana can limit _____ and impair thinking and learning skills.
21. _____ is an illegal drug that comes from the leaves of the hemp plant.
24. Sniffing the fumes of inhalants can cause damage to the body's _____ system.
25. Each year, careless smoking causes many _____.
26. The best defense against tobacco, alcohol, and other drugs may be learning to say _____.

Down

2. Buying tobacco products and alcohol is _____ for young teens.
3. Steroids can cause harmful side effects, including _____, sterility, and even death.
4. Breathing in smoke exhaled by smokers is known as _____ smoking.
5. Alcohol causes _____ to relax, which affects a drinker's ability to walk, talk, and drive a car.
9. Snuff and chewing tobacco are _____ tobacco products.
12. A strong physical need for a drug is known as an _____.
13. A concentrated form of cocaine is called _____.
15. Babies are more likely to be born _____ when their mothers smoke during pregnancy.
16. A white, powdery drug that is often sniffed through the nose is _____.
18. Alcohol is a major cause of _____ accidents and deaths.
20. Even drugs that have been _____ by a doctor can be harmful if they are not used correctly.
22. Many hospitals and clinics offer _____ programs for people seeking help to break habits with tobacco, alcohol, and other drugs.
23. Legal drugs that can be purchased without a prescription are called over-the-_____ drugs.

REST AND EXERCISE LOG

Activity D
Chapter 16

Name _____

Date _____ Period _____

Use this form to keep track of the amount of sleep you get each night for one week. Keep track of the types and amount of heavy exercise you get each day. Also note your overall energy level each day. At the end of the week, review the information you recorded in the chart. Then answer the questions at the bottom of the page.

	Sunday	Monday	Tuesday
Time of sleep			
Hours of sleep			
Type of heavy exercise			
Minutes of heavy exercise			
Overall energy level			

	Wednesday	Thursday
Time of sleep		
Hours of sleep		
Type of heavy exercise		
Minutes of heavy exercise		
Overall energy level		

	Friday	Saturday
Time of sleep		
Hours of sleep		
Type of heavy exercise		
Minutes of heavy exercise		
Overall energy level		

1. How does the amount of sleep you get seem to affect your energy level? _____

_____

2. What improvements could you make in your sleep habits? _____

_____

3. How does the amount of exercise you get seem to affect your energy level? _____

_____

4. What improvements could you make in your exercise habits? _____

_____

FACING CHANGE

GAINING INDEPENDENCE

Activity A
Chapter 17

Name _____

Date _____ Period _____

Interview a recent high school graduate on how increased independence has affected his or her lifestyle. Share your findings in class.

Age: _____

Gender: _____ Male _____ Female

1. How long have you been out of high school? _____

2. What is your current housing arrangement? (live with parents, live with roommate, college dorm, have own apartment, etc.) _____

3. Are you currently employed? _____

   If so, what type of work do you do? _____

   How many hours a week do you work? _____

4. What demands on your time do you have now that you did not have when you were younger?

   _____

   _____

5. What expenses do you have now that you did not have when you were younger? _____

   _____

6. Do you vote in local, state, and national elections? _____

7. What concerns do you have about the way the government spends your tax dollars? _____

   _____

   _____

8. What national and international events concern you most? _____

   _____

9. How has a more independent lifestyle affected your view of yourself? _____

   _____

10. In what ways do people treat you differently now that you are older and more independent?

    _____

    _____

11. What do you like most about your increased independence? _____

    _____

12. What do you find most challenging about a more independent lifestyle? _____

    _____

Activity B   Name _____

Chapter 17   Date _____ Period _____

Give suggestions to help each of the following teens adjust to the changes that are affecting his or her lifestyle.

Doreen: Having a baby sister is not as much fun as I thought it would be. In the daytime when she's sleeping, I have to be quiet. No one tells her to be quiet when her crying wakes me up in the middle of the night.

_____

_____

_____

Shane: It's kind of weird having my new stepfather around all the time. I don't know if I should treat him like a father, or like a friend, or what. I don't really know him very well yet.

_____

_____

_____

Ian: My grandmother moved in with us a few weeks ago. It's kind of a drag. She moves slowly and she's always talking about "the old days."

_____

_____

_____

Adrianne: We just moved into a house on the east side of the city. I have to go to a different school now. The new neighborhood seems nice, but I miss having my friends right next door.

_____

_____

_____

Jeffrey: My mom just started a new job with a downtown firm. It's a good opportunity for her. The only problem is, she has to leave at 6:30 to catch the morning train. She doesn't get back home until 7:00 in the evening. I don't mind doing more of the shopping and cooking for her. I just wish she could spend more time with me.

_____

_____

_____

SOURCES OF HELP

Activity C

Chapter 17

Name _____

Date _____ Period _____

For each crisis listed below, find the name and telephone number of a specific agency in your community to which people could turn for help.

CRISIS	SOURCES OF HELP	SPECIFIC RESOURCE
Unemployment	Psychologist Career counselor Financial counselor	
Divorce	Marriage counselor Lawyer Family counselor	
Running away	State department of family services Family counselor Runaway hot line	
Family violence	Social service organizations Family counselor	
Alcoholism	Alateen Alcoholism information and treatment centers	
Death/Suicide	Psychologist Suicide prevention center	

The following resource people can provide help in a variety of crisis situations. Give a specific name and telephone number for each person listed.

Teacher: _____

Religious leader: _____

Phone: _____

Phone: _____

School counselor: _____

Doctor: _____

Phone: _____

Phone: _____

Also list local phone numbers for the following:

Police department: _____

Hospital: _____

CRISIS PUZZLE

Activity D

Chapter 17

Name _____

Date _____ Period _____

Use terms and concepts from the chapter to help you fill in the word puzzle.

1.   _ _ _ F _ _ _ _ _ _ _ _
2.   _ _ A _ _
3.   _ _ _ C _ _ _
4.   _ _ I _ _ _
5.   _ _ N _ _ _ _ _
6. _ _ _ _ _ _ _ _ _ G
7.   _ _ _ _ _ C _
8.   _ _ _ _ H _ _ _ _
9.   _ _ _ _ _ _ A _
10.   _ _ _ _ _ _ N _ _
11.   _ _ G _ _ _ _
12.   _ E _ _ _ _

1. A family that does not function the way it should is called a _____ family.
2. A crisis that everyone must face at some point.
3. The act of a person who purposely kills himself or herself.
4. An event that has a great effect on a person's life.
5. Teenage _____ often become victims of crime and illness because they can't afford safe shelter and decent food.
6. Career and financial _____ can help families deal with unemployment.
7. The legal process of ending a marriage.
8. An addiction to alcohol.
9. The injury of one family member by another is called _____ abuse.
10. Purposely harming the self-concept of a family member is called _____ abuse.
11. Failure to provide a child with proper food, clothing, shelter, medical care, or supervision is called physical _____.
12. Forcing a family member to perform sex acts is called _____ abuse.

Chapter 18

LEADERS AND FOLLOWERS

———————— LEADERSHIP SKILLS ————————

Activity A

Chapter 18

Name _____

Date _____ Period _____

The following chart lists skills needed by group leaders. Complete the chart by filling in ways you would use each skill to lead a group. Then answer the questions below.

LEADERSHIP SKILL	IDEAS FOR DEVELOPING A SUCCESSFUL GROUP
Use knowledge	
Build interest	
Guide decisions	
Organize efforts	
Involve members	

1. What type of group would you like to lead? _____

2. What do you think would be the most challenging part of being a leader? _____

_____

3. What do you think you would enjoy most about being a leader? _____

_____

TAKING THE LEAD

Name _____

Date _____ Period _____

In the blanks below, list titles given to people in leadership positions that begin with each letter in the word *leaders*. Then describe how a leader might act in each of the situations that follow.

L _____

E _____

A _____

D _____

E _____

R _____

S _____

1. Many students have stopped buying the school newspaper. They complain about its lack of coverage of school events, poor organization, and wrong information. How could the editor use his or her skills to boost sales of the school newspaper?

_____

_____

2. Membership in the drama club has started to decline. How could the club president help to increase it?

_____

_____

3. The freshman class officers are disagreeing about the kind of fund-raising project they should have this year. Some of them want to hold a car wash. Others want to sell stationery. How could the class president help settle this dispute?

_____

_____

4. Confusion arose at a recent FHA awards ceremony. Some members arrived at 7:00 p.m. and others did not arrive until 7:30. Several members thought the meeting was being held in their regular classroom. However, most were sure the ceremony was taking place in the auditorium. Three different students brought flowers to present to the advisor on behalf of the group. How could the club president avoid this type of confusion in the future?

_____

_____

5. Last year, the pep club president was in charge of everything. She painted all the posters, made all the phone calls, and led all the rallies. Members started dropping out of the club because there was nothing for them to do. How can this year's president avoid this problem?

_____

_____

BEING A GROUP MEMBER

Activity C

Chapter 18

Name _____

Date _____ Period _____

Answer the following questions about a group in which you are involved. If you are not involved in a group, interview someone who is.

1. Name the group in which you are involved. _____

2. What is the purpose of the group? _____

3. What functions does the group perform to achieve its purpose? _____

   _____

4. How long has this group existed? _____

5. List and briefly describe the meanings of any special colors, symbols, or words used by the group.

   _____

6. What types of social events are held by the group? _____

7. How does the group raise money to support projects and activities? _____

   _____

8. What types of service projects does the group do? _____

9. How have you used your personal skills and talents to participate in the activities of this group?

   _____

10. What committees have you chaired and/or offices have you held? _____

11. What goals does your group have for this year? _____

12. Does your group follow parliamentary procedure? _____

    If not, how are meetings conducted? _____

13. Does your group use the decision-making process to set goals and plan projects? _____

    If not, how are group decisions made? _____

14. How does your group recruit new members? _____

    _____

15. How does your group advertise activities? _____

    _____

16. How are adults involved in your group? _____

    _____

17. How does your group recognize the efforts of individual members? _____

    _____

18. Briefly describe why being a member of this group has been important to you. _____

    _____

    _____

YOUR GROUP ROLE

Activity D

Chapter 18

Name _____

Date _____ Period _____

Evaluate your skills as a group member by checking all of the following statements that apply to you. Then answer the questions below.

LEADER

_____ I like to influence the thoughts of others.

_____ I like to be in charge.

_____ I like to finish projects once I start them.

_____ I like to complete tasks on time.

_____ I don't mind telling other people what to do.

_____ I can communicate instructions clearly.

_____ I enjoy sharing my knowledge with others so they can benefit from my experience.

_____ I can make decisions easily.

_____ I can set up schedules to organize people and events.

_____ I am willing to share responsibility with others rather than try to do everything myself.

FOLLOWER

_____ I don't mind having tasks assigned to me.

_____ I make it a point to learn the background about groups with which I am involved.

_____ I am willing to contribute my time to work on group projects and attend meetings.

_____ I enjoy sharing my talents with others.

_____ I don't mind doing little tasks like taking notes and making phone calls.

_____ I am not afraid to say what I think.

_____ I work well with others.

_____ I volunteer to help whenever I can.

_____ I try to stay informed about times, dates, and places of group events.

_____ I believe in doing my fair share of the work.

I am primarily: _____ A leader.   _____ A follower.

Why do you think leaders also need to have some of the characteristics of followers? _____

_____

Why do you think followers also need to have some of the skills of leaders? _____

_____

SHOW YOUR STRIPES

Activity E
Chapter 18

Name _____

Date _____ Period _____

On the stripes of the flag below, list ways people can demonstrate good citizenship.

THE ORDER OF BUSINESS

Activity F

Chapter 18

Name _____

Date _____ Period _____

Complete the two ordering exercises below. Place the letters of the corresponding events in the order of the numbered blanks. When completed, the letters in each exercise will spell out a word related to business meetings. Then answer the questions that follow.

I. A TYPICAL AGENDA

1. _____ U – Unfinished business.
2. _____ S – Adjournment.
3. _____ N – Committee reports.
4. _____ M – Call to order.
5. _____ T – New business.
6. _____ I – Officers' reports.
7. _____ E – Program.

II. MAKING A MOTION

8. _____ D – The leader asks for discussion of the motion.
9. _____ R – The leader recognizes the member by stating his or her name.
10. _____ R – The leader takes a vote on the motion.
11. _____ O – The member makes a brief, exact statement of the action he or she desires from the group.
12. _____ P – The member must get the attention of the group leader.
13. _____ U – Any member wishing to do so may ask questions or make comments about the motion.
14. _____ E – The president announces the decision.
15. _____ C – Another member seconds the motion.
16. _____ E – The leader repeats the motion.

17. How is an agenda helpful at a business meeting? _____

_____

_____

18. Why is following guidelines necessary when making motions?_____

_____

_____

114

A PLAN OF ACTION

Activity G

Chapter 18

Name _____

Date _____ Period _____

Work in a small group to form a plan of action for achieving one of the following goals. Share your plan in class.

GOAL A
The drama club has a goal to increase the number of people from the general public who attend their plays.
Suggested plans of action:
1. Involve the public in a school play.
2. Make tickets more available to the public.

GOAL B
The honors club has a goal to improve the visual image of the school.

Suggested plans of action:
1. Improve the appearance of the school grounds.
2. Redecorate the school lobby.

Our group will form a plan of action to achieve Goal _____.

Brainstorm for other possible plans of action. Write your ideas below.

3. _____
4. _____
5. _____

Our group has voted to follow plan of action number _____.

Steps for accomplishing the plan:

1. _____
2. _____
3. _____
4. _____
5. _____
6. _____
7. _____
8. _____

What committees will be formed to carry out the steps of the plan?

_____
_____
_____

How will your group evaluate your goal and your plan of action?

_____
_____

LEADERSHIP CROSSWORD

Name _____

Date _____ Period _____

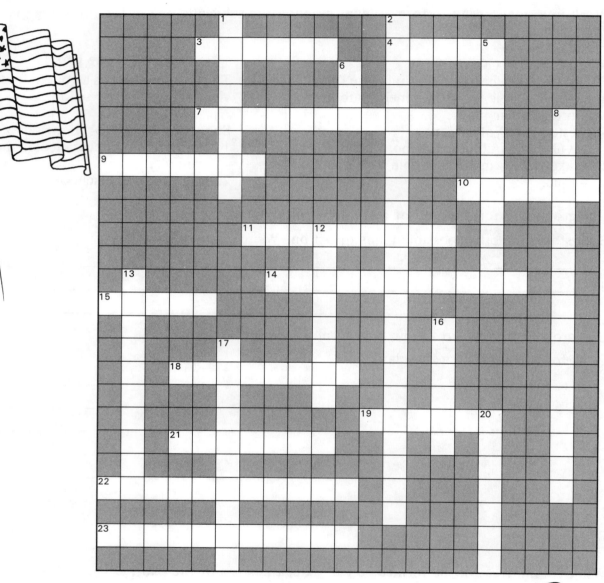

(Continued)

Name _____

Across

3. A _____ is a suggestion for a group to take action.
4. An _____ _____ committee disbands when its assigned task is finished.
7. _____ means working together to achieve common goals.
9. A _____ is someone who lives in a town, state, or country.
10. A group member must agree with, or _____, a motion before discussion can occur.
11. A _____ is a small group formed within the main group to do a certain task.
14. A group member moves for _____ to end the meeting.
15. Groups need to set and achieve _____ to give them direction.
18. A _____ is less than half of the members of a group.
19. Someone with the power to affect the thoughts and actions of others is a _____.
21. _____ are a record of what takes place at a meeting.
22. Unfinished business is followed by _____ _____, or issues that have not been discussed before.
23. _____ is the way citizens show loyalty to the governments of towns, states, and countries in which they live.

Down

1. Knowing how to be a good _____ is the responsibility of every group member.
2. _____ _____ is a method used by governments and organizations to conduct business.
5. A _____ is the leader of a committee.
6. _____ is a group for students in home economics classes.
8. A _____ _____ is a permanent committee.
12. Group decisions are determined by a _____.
13. Group members need to _____ their time, talents, and ideas to help a group reach its goals.
16. An _____ lists the order of events that will occur during a meeting.
17. _____ business refers to topics that have been discussed at an earlier meeting but still require a group decision.
20. A typical agenda includes _____ from officers and committee chairpersons.

SUCCESSFUL GROUPS

Activity I

Chapter 18

Name _____

Date _____ Period _____

Fill in the following lists of ways to make various school groups successful.

1. What special programs and events might require planning by the school choir?

_____
_____
_____
_____
_____
_____
_____

2. What unusual techniques might the science club use to advertise meetings and activities?

_____
_____
_____
_____
_____
_____
_____

3. What kinds of fun meetings and social events might be enjoyed by members of the Spanish club?

_____
_____
_____
_____
_____
_____

4. What kinds of fund-raising projects might the computer club choose to do?

_____
_____
_____
_____
_____
_____
_____

5. How might the marching band involve adults in the success of its program?

_____
_____
_____
_____
_____
_____
_____

6. What unusual awards might be given to recognize members of the drama club?

_____
_____
_____
_____
_____
_____

Chapter 19

GROWING THROUGH WORK

―――――――――――― THINKING ABOUT A CAREER ――――――――――

Activity A

Chapter 19

Name _____

Date _____ Period _____

Provide complete responses to the following questions or statements.

1. When you were a child, what kind of work did you think you wanted to do when you grew up?

   _____

2. List hobbies and school subjects that you enjoy.

   _____   _____

   _____   _____

   _____   _____

3. Do you prefer working with people, ideas, or objects? _____

4. What rewards do you hope to gain from your work? _____

   _____

5. Name an occupation and explain how it encompasses the interests identified by your answers to the previous questions. _____

   _____

   _____

6. Show how the occupation you listed in question #5 might fit into a series of occupations to form a career. List the entry-level position in the career by the lowest rung of the ladder below. List the position requiring the most skill and training by the highest rung. Fill in the other rungs with occupations that might serve as stepping stones for reaching the top position.

Activity B
Chapter 19

Name _____

Date _____ Period _____

Interview someone who works in a career area that interests you. Fill in his or her answers to the questions below.

Name: _____

Place of employment: _____

Job title: _____

1. How long have you worked for this employer? _____

2. What duties or tasks do you regularly perform as part of your job? _____

_____

_____

3. What job experience did you have before you began working in your present position?

_____

4. What educational level did you need to enter this career area? _____

5. What skills or training did you need to enter this career area? _____

_____

6. What kinds of companies or organizations hire people who work in this career area?

_____

_____

7. Do you belong to any unions or professional organizations related to your career? _____

   If so, how does membership in these unions or organizations help you in your career?

_____

_____

8. What is your weekly work schedule? _____

9. How much time do you get for daily lunch and coffee breaks? _____

_____

10. What, if any, overtime work are you required to do? _____

_____

11. What is a typical salary range for people working in this career area? _____

12. What opportunities for advancement are available in your position? _____

_____

13. What fringe benefits do you receive from your employer? _____

_____

14. How much paid vacation do you get each year? _____

15. How much paid sick leave do you get each year? _____

Activity C
Chapter 19

Name _____

Date _____ Period _____

Provide complete responses to the following questions or statements.

1. Check any of the following work traits that describe you.

_____ Able to accept criticism.   _____ Courteous.

_____ Respectful.   _____ Cooperative.

_____ Tolerant of differences.   _____ Willing to work hard and complete a job.

_____ Well groomed and suitably dressed. _____ Well organized.

_____ Able to communicate effectively.   _____ Cheerful.

_____ Adaptable.   _____ Honest.

_____ Enthusiastic.   _____ Dependable.

_____ Self-confident.   _____ Punctual.

_____ Willing to compromise.   _____ Assertive.

2. List tasks you do at home. Describe what work traits they are helping you to develop.

_____

_____

_____

3. List tasks you do at school. Describe what work traits they are helping you to develop.

_____

_____

_____

4. Describe any part-time jobs you have had or any volunteer work you have done. _____

_____

_____

5. Describe any computer skills you have and explain how you learned them._____

_____

_____

6. Do you feel that your work traits, job experience, and computer skills are helping to prepare you for a career? Explain why or why not._____

_____

_____

_____

WRITING A RESUME

Activity D　　　　　　　　Name _____

Chapter 19　　　　　　　　Date _____ Period _____

Make a rough draft of a resume by filling out the following form with information about yourself. Use the example on page 403 of the text as a guide. Have your teacher look at your rough draft and suggest how you might improve it. Then type a final draft on your own paper.

　　　　　　　　Name　　_____

　　　　　　　　Address　_____

　　　　　　　　*Phone no.*_____

JOB OBJECTIVE　_____

　　　　　　　　　_____

EDUCATION

Date _____　_____

　　　　　　　　　_____

　　　　　　　　　_____

WORK EXPERIENCE

Date _____　_____

　　　　　　　　　_____

Date _____　_____

　　　　　　　　　_____

HONORS AND

ACTIVITIES　　_____

　　　　　　　　　_____

REFERENCES　　_____

　　　　　　　　　_____

　　　　　　　　　_____

　　　　　　　　　_____

　　　　　　　　　_____

LETTER OF APPLICATION

Activity E
Chapter 19

Name _____

Date _____ Period _____

Identify the following types of want ads:

HELP WANTED
Local restaurant seeking cooks and buspersons to work evenings and weekends. Send resume to:
Fast & Friendly Restaurant
770 W. Willow Dr.
Washburn, IN 79840
Attn: Mr. Jacobs

1. _____

**PART TIME
DELIVERY HELP
WANTED**
Deliver flowers for local florist. Must have valid driver's license. Send resume to:
Box 326 Times
Washburn, IN 79840

2. _____

Write a letter of application in response to one of the above want ads. Use the example on page 409 of the text as a guide to formal business style. Use your own paper if you need more space.

_____
_____
_____
_____
_____
_____
_____
_____
_____
_____
_____
_____
_____
_____
_____
_____
_____
_____
_____
_____
_____
_____

THE INTERVIEW

Name _____

Date _____ Period _____

Amir, Roberta, and Jessie all interviewed for the following position advertised in the local paper:

> **PART-TIME BAKER'S ASST.**
> Afternoons and weekends.
> Contact bet. 1-5 p.m.
> Bunson's Bakery
> 114 W. Maple
> 555-3372

Read about each of their interviews and then answer the questions that follow.

AMIR. Amir's interview was scheduled for 3:00 p.m. He walked into the bakery at 2:45 wearing a clean, white shirt and freshly pressed slacks. His hair was neatly combed and his face and hands were clean.

During the first part of the interview, Amir told Mr. Bunson that he was honest and hardworking. He also mentioned that he'd been helping his mother bake breads and cakes since he was a little boy.

In the second half of the interview, Amir told Mr. Bunson that he could work only three afternoons and one weekend day each week. He also said that he was not available to work on Thursdays. He said he hoped to earn at least $6.00 an hour as he was trying to save money for college.

ROBERTA. Roberta's interview was scheduled for 3:30 p.m. At 3:35, Roberta hopped off of her bicycle and dashed into the bakery. Her hair and clothes were disheveled from her fast ride.

During the interview, Roberta confessed that she didn't have any baking experience. However, she enthusiastically told Mr. Bunson that she was willing to learn anything she needed to know.

Roberta said her schedule was free every afternoon and all weekend. She added that she would be interested in working full-time during the summer if Mr. Bunson needed her.

JESSIE. Jessie arrived right on time for her interview. She was neatly dressed in a bright red skirt with her fingernails painted to match.

At the beginning of the interview, Jessie mentioned that she was quite familiar with Bunson's Bakery. She said that her mother had been buying cookies and doughnuts there for years. Jessie told Mr. Bunson that, although she didn't have baking experience, she had worked as a waitress at Goldstein's Deli. She said she sometimes had meetings in the afternoons and plans on the weekends but her schedule was usually flexible.

Before the end of the interview, Mr. Bunson wanted to know if Jessie had any questions. Jessie asked whether or not a baker's assistant would be required to wear a uniform.

If you were Mr. Bunson, which applicant would you hire? Explain your choice. _____

_____

_____

What are your reasons for not selecting each of the other two applicants? _____

_____

_____

IS ENTREPRENEURSHIP FOR YOU?

Activity G
Chapter 19

Name _____

Date _____ Period _____

Read the following statements. Place a check in the column that best describes your opinion. Then answer the questions at the bottom of the page.

	Agree	Disagree	Unsure
1. I like taking risks.	_____	_____	_____
2. I would be interested in learning about how to operate a business.	_____	_____	_____
3. I am a good time manager.	_____	_____	_____
4. I am a good money manager.	_____	_____	_____
5. I am a good leader.	_____	_____	_____
6. I like to make my own decisions.	_____	_____	_____
7. Completing tasks on my own gives me a feeling of success.	_____	_____	_____
8. I don't mind long hours of hard work.	_____	_____	_____
9. I enjoy handling big responsibilities.	_____	_____	_____
10. I don't mind handling numerous, little tasks.	_____	_____	_____
11. I would be willing to invest my own money in a business venture.	_____	_____	_____
12. I can identify a needed product or service that I could provide for potential customers in my area.	_____	_____	_____

What do your answers tell you about your interest in becoming an entrepreneur?

_____

_____

If you were to become an entrepreneur, what type of product or service would you like to sell?

_____

_____

What do you think you'd like most about being an entrepreneur?

_____

_____

What do you think you'd like least about being an entrepreneur?

_____

_____

Activity H

Chapter 19

Name _____

Date _____ Period _____

The following sentences contain coded terms from the chapter. Use the example and the defini-tions to break the code. Then decode the mystery message below.

Example: J O B   S E A R C H
          C A N   E M P L O Y

1. A well-written _ _ _ _ _ _ clearly presents a person's job qualifications to an employer.
   L M E D Z M

2. Although they don't get paid for it, _ _ _ _ _ _ _ _ _ work helps teens gain job experience.
   J A W D H R M M L

3. An _ _ _ _ _ _ _ _ _ _ _ is someone who starts and manages a business.
   M H R L M S L M H M D L

4. An entry-level worker who learns a trade from skilled workers is an
   _ _ _ _ _ _ _ _ _ _.
   P S S L M H R X O M

5. In most states, a young teen who wishes to work outside the home is required to get a
   _ _ _ _ _ _ _ _ _.
   Q A L V S M L Z X R

6. Someone an employer can call to ask about a person's capabilities as a worker is a
   _ _ _ _ _ _ _ _.
   L M B M L M H O M

7. Working during the teen years can help people gain the _ _ _ _ _ _ _ _ _ they need for employment as adults.
   M F S M L X M H O M

8. Meeting with an employer in an _ _ _ _ _ _ _ _ _ gives an applicant a chance to discuss his or her job qualifications.
   X H R M L J X M Q

9. For tax and identification purposes, all workers need _ _ _ _ _ _
   E A O X P W
   _ _ _ _ _ _ _ numbers.
   E M O D L X R T

10. A job _ _ _ _ _ _ _ _ _ is a brief statement on a resume about the kind of work a person is seeking.
   A N C M O R X J M

Mystery Message: _ _ _ _ _ _ _   _   _ _ _   _ _ _ _ _ _ _
                     U M R R X H U   P   C A N   L M K D X L M E

_ _ _ _ '   _ _ _ _ _ _ _ '   _ _ _   _ _ _ _ _ _ _.
E V X W W   V H A Q W M G U M   P H G   U D Z S R X A H